Democracy and Reform
in Public Schools

Democracy and Reform in Public Schools

The Case for Collaborative Partnerships

Saul Rubinstein
Charles Heckscher
John McCarthy

HARVARD EDUCATION PRESS
CAMBRIDGE, MASSACHUSETTS

Paperback ISBN 978-1-68253-850-0

Library of Congress Cataloging-in-Publication Data is on file.

Published by Harvard Education Press,
an imprint of the Harvard Education Publishing Group

Harvard Education Press
8 Story Street
Cambridge, MA 02138

Cover Design: Endpaper Studio
Cover Image: Andriy Onufriyenko/Moment via Getty Images

The typefaces in this book are Scala and Scala Sans.

To my wife, Karen, my mother, Mae, and my daughter, Gabrielle,
who inspire this work through their example and commitment
to elevating voice and the values of democracy

—SAUL RUBINSTEIN

To my daughter, Fiona, a dedicated collaborator
and teacher in schools and in all aspects of life

—CHARLES HECKSCHER

To Sandra, John, Heather, and Matthew. I am forever grateful.

—JOHN MCCARTHY

Contents

PART I

The Challenge of Educational Reform

P ART I OF THIS BOOK traces the decades-long history of neoliberal public school reform in the United States and explores why these polices have not produced the results promised. It then outlines an alternative approach to improvement and reform, one based on multi-stakeholder partnerships between school boards, teacher unions, and administrators that produce more collaborative systems in public schools with improved outcomes for students and educators.

In part II we present research that shows the effectiveness of Collaborative Partnerships—combining extensive internal participation in decision-making with partnership among the major stakeholders—for improving teaching and learning, including increases in student achievement and reductions in teacher turnover, among other benefits, especially in high-poverty schools.

Part III reviews a century-long trend of increasing collaboration in corporations, driven by the challenges of growing complexity and pace of change faced by almost all organizations. It also describes some long-running and successful examples of Collaborative Partnership in public education and the changing roles of unions engaged in these systems.

In part IV we describe the development of a Public School Collaborative network in New Jersey, which has drawn on these experiences for a model that has over the past decade expanded to twenty-five public school districts. We particularly focus on key elements that have helped to create an unusually robust and resilient system that can be used in other states and could be scaled for a transformative approach to public education.

CHAPTER 1

The Debate over the Future of US Public School Reform

FOR DECADES, motivated by comparisons of US public school student performance against international benchmarks, a debate has raged across the country regarding the best way to reform and improve US K–12 public education. Surprisingly, Democrats and Republicans have been mainly on the same side in this debate, even while they have been able to agree on little in other policy areas: they have steadily supported a mix of school choice—through charter schools and vouchers—and mandated high-stakes testing overseen and enforced by government. This approach deeply undermines the system of public education established throughout the country over the past century and a half. Despite support by both parties over six administrations, the approach has consistently failed to produce the promised outcomes.

This chapter examines those public school reform policies and proposes an alternative. We begin with a review of education reform in the United States, starting with the influence of mass production management philosophies on the relationships of administrators and teachers. We then examine and critique the specific neoliberal reforms advanced by both Republican and Democratic administrations over the past forty years. This is followed by the introduction of an alternative approach to public school reform rooted in new organizational and institutional relationships (partnerships) among teacher unions, administrations, and school boards that facilitates collaboration among the key stakeholders and has led to improved student achievement in public schools across the country.

THE INFLUENCE OF SCIENTIFIC MANAGEMENT

Public schools in the United States today continue to carry the legacy of bureaucratic principles of management developed more than a century ago and pushed to the ultimate degree by Frederick Taylor. Taylor clearly differentiated the work of management (planning and thinking) from that of labor (implementing management's plans). His *Principles of Scientific Management*, published in 1911, was heralded by many scholars and education leaders as an objective, scientifically grounded means by which to ensure that teachers and teaching methods were efficient and that the materials students were taught complied with standards.[1] Some drew explicit analogs between schooling and factory work, viewing children as the raw materials to be molded by teachers to meet the needs of society, as if progressing along an assembly line.[2]

Just as "scientific management" in manufacturing attempted to separate labor from decisions regarding the appropriate method of work, scientific management in schools attempted to remove or minimize teachers' influence over important matters regarding children's education.[3] Matters of curriculum development were believed to be too complex to be left to teachers or laypeople who were unfamiliar with popular managerial theory: "Only those who had studied the textbooks, read the research, taken the courses, and mastered the theories could be permitted to decide what children should learn," as well as how they should learn it.[4] In the model envisioned by proponents of scientific management in education, administrators worked to develop the best curriculum, learning materials, instructional plans, and metrics for evaluation and then passed these guidelines on to teachers, who were expected to faithfully carry them out. This policy of applying industrial techniques to education spread quickly. Principals took on the role of middle managers. Superintendents assumed an executive role, establishing curriculum, instructional practices, and standardized metrics for evaluating performance throughout the district as a whole.

Throughout the twentieth century, the scientific management efficiency movement attempted to transition teachers from philosophers of education, actively engaged in determining what should be taught and how to teach it, to passive instruments for fulfilling whatever pedagogical techniques were laid down from on high.[5] Knowledge was channeled into ever-smaller areas, divided by classrooms, and deemed valuable only insofar as it bore association with defined, measurable outcomes.[6] Unsurprisingly, teacher opposition bubbled to the surface. Teachers objected to the Tayloristic standardization of their craft not only because it undermined their agency as professional educators but because it miscalculated what was of value, emphasizing cost per student and a quantifiable gain at the expense of what was less tangible but nonetheless important.

THE NEOLIBERAL NARRATIVE

In the late twentieth century, school reform became driven by a combination of Taylorist views about teachers and the free-market theories of neoliberalism. Schools were no longer thought of as just factories but also as businesses subject to market forces. Neoliberalism is a worldview that holds that everyone is better off when markets operate freely, so that people can pursue their own self-interest unfettered by government regulations. Neoliberals believe in minimizing the state's role, except where government is necessary to protect free markets.

The past forty years of school reform policy, refined over six administrations—both Republican and Democrat—have been built on this neoliberal ideology about the importance of free markets in public education through expanding the use of charter schools, vouchers, and privatization. The theory was that competition among different models, driven by parental choice, would lead to steady improvement of the "product." Like corporations, schools have become more market-focused externally but more bureaucratic internally, characterized by a rigid hierarchy that reduces the discretion exercised by employees by setting explicit standards for each task and job and then ensuring adherence to those standards through supervisors.

With its roots in Taylorism, this neoliberal approach operates under the "assumption that if [educators] adhere to the rules—teaching the prescribed curriculum, maintaining the correct class sizes, using the appropriate text-books, and accumulating the right number of course credits—students will learn what they need to know."[7] Decision-making about core issues under this model is removed from those who carry out the task of teaching, while student learning and teacher effectiveness are viewed as being distillable to a set of core criteria that can be precisely measured and used for evaluation and comparison. In seeking to expose public schools to the forces of the competitive marketplace, the neoliberal approach assumes that the problem with US public education is the withheld discretionary effort by teachers that results from a lack of accountability, incentives, and pressure; in other words, teachers are blamed for any failures of the education system, and the solution is to exert greater control over them.[8] With greater competition through charter schools, vouchers, and privatization, neoliberals hope to provide less job security for teachers and therefore assume that they will be motivated to work harder and more effectively. Public schools that lag behind must improve or risk closure. Charter schools are seen to hold special promise because they operate outside the restrictive policies of the public bureaucracy and accompanying union rules.[9]

But there is a contradiction at the heart of this neoliberal narrative for education: neither party really sees education as simply a matter of individual choice; both see it as also a national priority, essential to preserving US competitiveness and pursuing the basic value of equal opportunity for all. Therefore, education requires national standards of performance.

Instead of leading to simple decentralization, policies have simultaneously centralized the power of testing and evaluation.

The result has been a sustained effort to define standards of educational achievement and to hold schools accountable for them through competition, tests, and strong sanctions for failure to meet the standards. Again, both parties have pursued this line with equal enthusiasm.

In public school reform, the shift to standards and outcomes (test results) and away from a focus on ensuring adequate resources, particularly for high-poverty schools, fails to recognize the impact of poverty on student achievement. In addition, teachers are held accountable through monitoring their compliance with standards and measuring outcomes, thereby further reducing their professional voice and agency.

This legacy of top-down reform that limited teacher voice as professional educators can be found in the reforms put forward by all administrations over the past four decades. During Ronald Reagan's first term in office, his administration created a National Commission on Excellence in Education that produced the famous 1983 report *A Nation at Risk: The Imperative for Educational Reform*. This report claimed underachievement by US students on comparative international standardized tests and warned that American education had been "eroded by a rising tide of mediocrity that threatens our very future as a Nation and a people."[10] Reagan then leveraged this claim to enact legislation that expanded the collection and use of comparative student test data from the National Assessment of Educational Progress (NAEP). It argued that substandard student achievement was a global risk to the United States both economically and socially. While questions were raised about the validity of the research behind the report, the Reagan administration nonetheless used it to set the stage for a new national education reform agenda by pushing for higher standards in US K–12 education, for expanded use of tests nationwide to measure achievement, and for greater use of private sector business and free-market approaches through more parental choice in their children's schools.[11]

Since the publication of *A Nation at Risk*, the growing perception in the United States has been that the country's education system has veered sharply off course and that decisive involvement by the federal government is necessary to help the system gain its competitive bearings. Active federal involvement in school reform increased momentum in the late 1980s under the presidency of George H. W. Bush, who continued support for these educational policies in concert with state leaders across the country, including then-governor Bill Clinton. Bush's efforts began with the National Educational Goals of 1989, which included school readiness, graduation goals, and subject-matter proficiency. Pushed further by private-sector business advocates, the Bush administration argued, in its America 2000 proposal of 1991, for increased voluntary standards and testing and for private school choice through vouchers. The proposal failed to gain congressional approval over several issues, including school choice; however, it further shaped the framing of US public school reform around the issues of standards, testing, accountability, and choice.

The Clinton administration continued this trajectory through the Goals 2000: Educate America Act and the Improving America's Schools Act, which established national standards, pressured states through funding to adopt aligned standards and tests, and required school and district accountability through report cards analyzed by states to determine progress for all students, as well as disadvantaged students, against these standards. These policy initiatives also shifted the question of educational equity away from differences in access to resources and toward providing equitable standards and curriculum. An important alliance for this reform strategy emerged between the entrepreneurs within the business community and other advocates of free-market approaches and civil rights leaders including the NAACP and liberals concerned with equity issues. Charters, in particular, were seen as a way to give children in underserved communities a higher-quality education.

This public school reform agenda intensified under the administration of George W. Bush. His No Child Left Behind (NCLB) law passed the House and Senate with overwhelming bipartisan support in 2001. This legislation called for testing every child in both math and reading in grades 3 through 8 and again in high school. By 2007, science testing was to be introduced. States could develop their own standards and choose their own tests, but schools had to show "Adequate Yearly Progress" with 100 percent grade-level proficiency in reading and math by 2014. As a first step for forcing accountability, students could transfer to another school if schools did not meet yearly goals. If a school continued to "fail," corrective action would be taken by changing curriculum, increasing teaching hours, and/or firing faculty and administration. As a final punitive step, if schools did not improve sufficiently, they could be closed, turned into charter schools with private management, or taken over by the state.

Charter schools receive public funding but are run independently of the public school district by private management organizations or community-based groups. They typically have no publicly elected school boards and operate for the most part without teacher unions. Charters are also exempt from many of the state regulations and laws that govern public schools. Thus, market reform advocates believed that the choice parents could make to move their children out of public schools and into charters would discipline the public schools to improve. They also believed that turning over public education to private management organizations would improve education through privatization—managing schools privately with public dollars.

Bush was also a proponent of another market-based reform—vouchers. Vouchers are publicly funded scholarships that parents can use to send their children to private or parochial schools. It was believed this choice by parents would again create another market in which public schools would be in competition with private schools, forcing public schools to improve or face the prospect of having no students. NCLB rested on the reform logic that the problem with education was inadequate expectations and accountability. Thus, setting high standards and well-articulated goals, along with greater monitoring through standardized tests and private sector competition, would improve student outcomes across the board. Bush expanded the federal role in education by pushing this agenda of reform through rigid standards, testing-based accountability, and parental choice. The testing regime introduced by NCLB became law across the country.

Barack Obama's secretary of education, Arne Duncan, put Bush's NCLB reforms on steroids. The Obama administration's Race to the Top (RTTT) program created an intense competition for $4.35 billion in postrecession 2009 stimulus funding. To compete for these funds, states had to change their laws and education policies to improve standards, expand the use of student testing, and use those results to evaluate teachers and hold them accountable for student performance (value-added assessments), as well as to increase competition through the use of charter schools. Thirty-four states, the District of Columbia, and Puerto Rico had to modify their education laws and policies in order to be eligible to submit reform plans and receive funding under RTTT. Forty-six states and the District of Columbia put together RTTT reform plans, but only eighteen received funding. Thus, Duncan used the leverage of this funding (less than 1 percent of total US school spending) to change education policies and laws across the country to increase the usage of common standards and high-stakes testing for students, to introduce punitive accountability measures through the use of these tests in teacher evaluations and in the decisions to close schools, and to expand charter schools and vouchers.

Continuing to promote these policies, Donald Trump's secretary of education, Betsy DeVos, worked hard to expand school choice and privatization, especially through the use of vouchers.

In sum, the reforms outlined above, which were promoted from Reagan through Trump but pursued most aggressively by the Bush administration's NCLB and its better-funded cousin, Obama's RTTT, were all neoliberal approaches to education reform combining free-market policies (charters and vouchers) with an increased managerial emphasis on standards, testing, control, and bureaucratic accountability measures.

Neither NCLB nor RTTT was research based; there were no studies or evidence that these approaches would work. Instead, these reforms were pushed because of ideology—that markets would produce better results than the public sector and that student achievement would improve if schools were privately managed (not necessarily by educators) and rooted in more corporate businesslike practices. This approach also meant less democratic governance, because charter, private, and for-profit schools operate without publicly elected school boards and typically do not have teacher unions.

A Lack of Results

Despite their popularity with policy makers, these neoliberal approaches to school reform not only have undermined the system of public education and had a negative impact on school climate by undervaluing teachers—dismissing their professional input and attacking their unions—but have also failed to produce the promised results. They have not raised test scores; NAEP scores have been flat over this forty-year period.[12] Overall, a variety of studies have shown that charter schools on average have not performed any better than public schools.[13] Further, evaluation of charter performance also suffers from a selection bias: compared with their public counterparts, charters often have more-involved families and more-motivated students, enroll proportionately fewer students with learning disabilities or who are English language learners (ELLs), and have fewer students with discipline issues. Concluding that charters were not producing equity by closing the achievement gap, the NAACP in 2016 abandoned its support for charters and called for a moratorium on their further expansion. The research on voucher programs has demonstrated that they actually produced worse results for students.[14]

A 2016 evaluation of RTTT by the US Department of Education itself could not determine whether the reforms it promoted had any impact on student test scores despite the multibillion-dollar investment.[15] In 2018, the RAND Corporation and the American Institutes of Research studied the value-added assessment program that the Department of Education, the Gates Foundation, and others had promoted to evaluate teachers based on student test scores. The research found that this costly reform had no impact on teaching quality or student achievement.[16] By then, nearly all states that had adopted the two national common core standards tests pushed by Duncan—Partnership for Assessment of Readiness for College and Careers (PARCC) and Smarter Balanced Assessment Consortium—had reversed course and dropped them.

Not only were the results poor; the punitive accountability measures adopted by NCLB and even more intensively by RTTT had exacted huge costs. Billions of dollars had been spent on testing, the creation of new standards and related curriculum, the purchase of new educational materials, new systems of teacher evaluation, and school closures. Further, since only reading and math were tested, other subjects were cut, de-emphasized, or received reduced instruction time. In the meantime, educators had been vilified by NCLB and RTTT and demoralized by the reform movement's value-added testing regime that wasted teaching time on extensive testing and test preparation. Teachers began leaving the profession at the fastest rate on record, and as teacher shortages increased, this assault made it even more difficult to attract young people to the teaching profession.[17] And worse, the legacy of the neoliberal reforms of RTTT—increased testing, accountability through evaluation and school closures, and attempts to institute market discipline through charters and vouchers—were now written into law in a majority of states thanks to the leverage exercised by Duncan.

In addition, neoliberal reform policies have created friction between teacher unions, administrators, school boards, parents, policy makers, and other stakeholders in public education and have fueled disagreements over how to improve the quality of teaching and learning for children. While many factors make consensus elusive when it comes to school reform, a key obstacle to finding agreement around educational improvements and bringing such improvements to fruition has been strained relations among the key stakeholders, particularly teacher unions and administration.

As we write in 2022, a sense of crisis hangs over the education sector. Student performance has dropped widely and deeply during the prior two pandemic years. Conflict has erupted in many states—among administrators, governments, parents, school boards, and teachers—over safety protocols and curricular approaches to race and gender. The key stakeholders are increasingly at loggerheads. And the bipartisan unity around the neoliberal agenda has disintegrated.

AN ALTERNATIVE FRAMEWORK FOR REFORM: COLLABORATIVE PARTNERSHIP

The neoliberal model is attractive because it appears to resolve major tensions in the system of public education. On one hand, there is a need for consistency in the core skills of citizens and in their understanding of civic traditions and institutions. On the other, parents increasingly want input into what is taught. The neoliberal resolution of this tension is to say that parents are free to shape education in private and religious schools, but all public school students have to meet performance standards that are consistent across the nation.

The essential problem, however, is that this model creates increasing tension between the parents, who have been told they are free to shape their own education system and government regulators charged with enforcing uniformity. Teachers, who actually deliver the education to children, are caught in the middle, their discretion limited by conflicting parental demands and government requirements, while the top-down legacy of Tayloristic control is reinforced by the pressure from constant high-stakes testing. Rather than developing alignment, this constellation of forces increases fragmentation and conflict. So it is not surprising that neoliberalism produces disappointing results.

Running against the neoliberal current, a number of school systems have developed an alternative: they bring together key stakeholders in Collaborative Partnerships focused on developing shared approaches to the improvement of teaching and learning.

This approach to reform starts with a basic shift in mentality: it trusts teachers to work with administrators and communities around shared goals. It is based on a perspective that values the legitimacy of multiple stakeholders in our public school systems—school boards, administrators, teacher unions, faculty and staff, parents, and students.[18] The approach values input, dialogue, and improvement through joint problem-solving, decision-making, and implementation. It represents an alternative to the approach of top-down standards and high-stakes testing.

This collaborative approach is not just a theoretical construct: it has been developed through decades of experience in many school districts around the country. But they have remained isolated and scattered in the face of the national neoliberal current, never coalescing in a coherent model that can be applied on a large scale. The aim of this book is to sketch such a model based on the experiences so far.

But what exactly *is* this "collaborative approach"? Since there is no clear consensus on the meaning of these words, we need to clarify our focus of interest in this book.

Collaboration, as the word is commonly used in organizations, is the participation of employees in problem-solving and decision-making in order to advance shared purposes. There are many varieties and gradations, from informal conversations between managers and their employees, to elaborate teams bringing together many players with differing skills and knowledge.[19]

We add to this the concept of multi-stakeholder *partnership*, which brings independent institutions into the process. Union-management partnerships are the most familiar form. Our work includes partnerships bringing together not just administrators and unions but other strategic stakeholders as well. The New Jersey Public School Collaborative, which will be our primary focus, has been supported by a group of leaders from the teacher unions and state associations of school boards, superintendents, principals and supervisors. These groups have brought independent perspectives to the effort and have engaged their own members to build trust and support.

Collaboration thus refers to participation in problem-solving and participation *within* an organization; *partnership* refers to a cooperative relationship among *independent* stakeholder organizations.

We have evidence (presented in the chapters that follow) that partnership can add power to collaborative systems, making them even more effective and innovative. Hence we will use a hybrid term for the model we propose: *Collaborative Partnership.*

Collaboration can exist without partnership. Many businesses and other organizations have developed participatory cultures that engage workers in problem-solving without changing the basic governance structure. This can be very informal and can lead to good harmony. But collaboration of this kind is vulnerable to changes in leadership, and it is not good at generating alignment for significant *improvements* in the organization.

On the other hand, partnership can exist without collaboration. Most union-management partnerships have been of this type: they consist of committees in which union representatives and managers jointly make decisions in specific areas, such as health and safety. Many European countries still have a strong role for joint labor-management groups in factory governance, a system known as "works councils." But these have largely been an institution at the enterprise level, and they rarely engage large numbers of rank-and-file workers directly.

Other types of partnership have similarly lacked a participatory element. Business partnerships between companies rarely engage the parties' employees, including middle managers, and for that reason they often run into problems of implementation when those employees need to work together. Social partnerships with environmental or other social-value groups have the same issue: these are almost always driven by specialized functions in the corporate headquarters and fail to engage the employees needed to make the partnerships function.

In Collaborative Partnerships, by contrast, the core strategic stakeholders in the partnering organizations engage closely with those who need to implement the strategies. The two elements can create a synergy in which the engagement of members of the partner organizations stimulates innovation and commitment, while the partners provide resources and a framework of stability for the system as a whole.

This model has been developing slowly in education and other organizations over the past fifty years. Partnership provides institutional and structural scaffolding for collaboration: rather than relying on the attitudes of particular administrators who can change over time, it creates a set of improvement teams and joint committees that are able to survive changes in leadership.

This alternative approach is problem-focused, bringing all resources to bear on finding solutions instead of trying to use market forces to compete with and "discipline" public schools into improvement or subjecting them to enforced top-down testing. Resources are devoted to bringing professionals together to find new and better ways to educate instead of spending on more and higher-stakes testing.

True collaboration also requires decision-making processes that are widely distributed rather than reserved for a small subset of managers. Of course, this is never a total shift: no organization can function by hashing through every decision collectively, and authority always remains an important element. What collaborative organizations add is the capability to take important decisions into a different forum, where all stakeholders can express their perspectives and work toward a solution that is supported by all. Shared decision-making also encourages clarity and agreement about what the collective aspires to accomplish and widespread commitment to seeing it through.

Collaborative Partnership involves a shift in the drivers of education reform: from markets to multiple stakeholders; from testing to teaching and learning; from policy makers in Washington, DC, and statehouses to district and school educators; from a command-and-control perspective to one based on partnership and collaboration; from a top-down approach to believing the answers are in the room or in the school (see table 1.1).

Unlike the neoliberal policies discussed earlier, our work in the sphere of K–12 education is based on actual data, which we will elaborate in part II. We know from many studies of manufacturing that effective participation

TABLE 1.1   The Collaborative Partnership approach shifts the drivers of education reform

	From →	To
What?	Markets	Multiple stakeholders
	Testing	Teaching and learning
Who?	Policymakers	Educators and communities
How?	Command and control	Partnership and collaboration
	Top-down	Answer in the room

leads to performance improvements. Along with other colleagues, we have extended this research to education, showing that collaboration yields significant improvements in school performance. One strand of this research has been quantitative, through analyses of schools and districts across the country. These studies have shown that districts with Collaborative Partnerships

- are significantly better on average than noncollaborative ones in terms of student achievement;
- are dramatically better in terms of improved teacher retention and commitment, *especially* in high-poverty districts;
- foster rich networks of communication among educators across schools and districts, largely coordinated by local union representatives, helping to generate and sustain innovation; and
- lead to transformations in the roles of administrators and union leaders, who are seen more as resources for learning and support than as taskmasters and fighters.

These findings are further supported by a long history of experience of collaboration and partnership, not only in education but in many other sectors, which we discuss in part III. Some important union-management partnerships have supported deep collaboration on the shop floor—especially in the automobile, steel, health care, and telecommunications industries.

These efforts have required difficult changes. Unions were originally created as oppositional bodies to balance the growing power of bureaucratic managers, and the entire legal framework of labor relations is based on this adversarial concept. Just as managers are often wedded to a mentality of bureaucratic control, union leaders are often focused on building oppositional strength. We have seen in many of these cases, however, that true union-management partnership in the governance of the work process can improve both the effectiveness of organizations and the quality of work life, and thereby strengthen both parties. Our deeper qualitative research of examples of sustained Collaborative Partnerships in education, such as the long-running effort in the ABC Unified School District in California, which we have studied in depth, have shown the same basic points.

Many of these efforts have been hard to sustain, often because of conflict with outside stakeholders or because new leaders have gone back to more familiar ways of behaving. But when such efforts succeed, they can be transformative. The successes have shown the importance of key elements across all cases, including a focus on substantive areas affecting the quality of teaching and student achievement—the shared purpose that unites all stakeholders; processes for building trust, among leaders and throughout the district; and recognizing education reform as a systems problem, involving culture, processes, and formal structure. These efforts also teach us the need for steady development over time, constructing the pieces of a new system as participants are ready rather than imposing rigid templates. These are some of the foundations of the model we will develop in part IV.

CONCLUSION

The collaborative approach to school reform has been tested in practice and by rigorous research and has shown itself to be a viable alternative to the neoliberal policies of the past. While neoliberalism has its roots in the ideology of free-market managerialism, collaborative school reform is rooted in *multi-stakeholder institutional pluralism.* Its democratic values are combined with twenty-first century organizational and employment relations practices. As state-level unions, school boards, and administrator associations work together to scale this approach, they are building on the US tradition of states as "Laboratories of Democracy."

PART II

The Research Base

THE NEXT TWO CHAPTERS develop the evidence, from our own research and others', that Collaborative Partnerships benefit students, teachers, and schools. Recall from chapter 1 that our basic argument is in two parts: collaboration is beneficial, but collaboration bolstered by institutional partnerships is even better.

To date, there are very few published studies dealing with collaborative school reform efforts that have a broad focus on the improvement of the overall operations of districts, from the school board to the classroom, including teaching and student performance. Our work attempts to fill that gap by exploring the impact of extensive collaboration between teachers and administrators, sustained over time by institutional partnerships. Our research is also unique in analyzing how these partnerships emerged, were structured, contributed to school quality, and endured over long periods.

This chapter develops evidence for the first argument by showing that collaboration is associated with

- improvements in student achievement, in high-poverty districts as well as wealthier ones; and
- improved teacher morale and reduced turnover, *especially* in high-poverty districts.

The next chapter will explore the effects of partnership in broadening and strengthening communication networks and encouraging innovation.

CHAPTER 2

The Impact of Collaboration on Student Achievement and Teacher Turnover

THE APPROACH we propose has two equally important compo-
nents: *collaboration* and *partnership*. *Collaboration* takes place within
organizations: we define it as the participation of members of an organization
in decision-making. *Partnership* takes place across organizations: it consists
of the engagement of independent stakeholders. Our findings indicate
that collaboration improves organizational performance, and partnership
enhances that effect. The two have a synergistic relation, each strengthening the other. We separate them here, somewhat artificially—focusing on
the effects of collaboration in this chapter and on the added contribution
of partnership in the next.

In schools, collaboration can involve many employees of the organization,
such as maintenance workers, technical staff, and office staff. But we focus
here primarily on the participation of teachers. Scholars suggest that the
most sought-after outcome for education moving forward should be systems
that promote commitment, continued learning, and informed experimentation among highly trained professionals.[1] Most schools work under the
assumption that what is designed and forcefully implemented from the top

will be faithfully carried out by those in the classroom. However, research and experience show that successful, sustained improvement requires that educators be committed to the goals and strategies that will be collectively undertaken.[2] This means that teachers should have a *voice* in decisions regarding curriculum, how standards will be used, which instructional practices and learning materials will be incorporated, and how assessments will be implemented, so as to encourage shared goals and decisions that educators are committed to carrying out.[3]

Collaboration is often equated with niceness—everyone getting along—or, in the social science terminology, a good organizational climate. That is not what we mean by collaboration. On the contrary, we expect collaborative systems to be full of robust debates and disagreements. What is distinctive about collaboration is that these debates are focused on improving the effectiveness of teaching and learning rather than on the comfort of administrators, teachers, and other stakeholders. A merely "nice" culture may be more pleasant than one riven by internal squabbles, but it is not likely to produce significant new ideas for performance improvement.

Effective collaborative systems are characterized by shared, overlapping goals; shared responsibilities and processes for planning, problem-solving, and decision-making; open exchange of information; and high levels of trust. These components interconnect. Trust is rooted in whether people feel they can rely on others to help create shared value. It is bolstered by norms of interdependence and mutual support. Goals define what the collective aims to accomplish over manageable time frames.

We have found solid evidence that collaboration is connected to significant improvements in student performance and other outcomes, and *when it is done right*, these improvements are dramatic. Some of the strongest results were found at one of the best cases of collaboration, the ABC Unified School District in Southern California, which we have studied closely. We have also found supportive evidence from our studies of a large set of districts across the country. Finally, we review the work of other researchers who have shown significant positive relationships and causal chains between collaboration and performance.

COLLABORATION IS LINKED TO IMPROVED STUDENT PERFORMANCE

Our research shows a significant link between collaboration and student performance in two major studies: a deep dive into a district where some schools (but not all) had a long history of strong collaboration, and a broad survey of 450 schools across the nation.

The ABC Unified School District

Our research into the links between institutional partnership, collaboration quality, and student performance began with the ABC Unified School District.[4] The ABC District is one of the longest-running union-management partnerships that school district leaders developed in the mid-1990s, and it is an extraordinary district in terms of challenges and successes. The district is large, with 1,100 educators serving 21,000 students in thirty schools, including nineteen elementary schools, five middle schools, five high schools, and an adult school that offers remedial education and career development for older students. At the time of the study, nearly half of the schools were Title I schools—schools that receive federal funds to support their high percentages of students from low-income families. More than 45 percent of the district's students were eligible for the free or reduced-price lunch program, and 25 percent of the students were English language learners. Despite these challenges, the students in this district consistently scored above state averages in student achievement tests.

This district offers a rare test for our approach because it is one of the few that has implemented Collaborative Partnership in schools over a sustained period of time. In addition, there was substantial variance in the degree of collaboration—that is, of teacher participation in problem-solving and decision-making—across schools, so we can see whether the more collaborative schools generally have higher student achievement.

We measured the strength of each school's collaboration using a survey that asked teachers to report the degree to which they communicated with one another, shared in the development of school plans and initiatives, and had a voice in decision-making with school administrators.

The responses to these questions gave us a collaboration metric. Schools that had higher levels of collaboration were schools where there was more teacher-administrator communication and information sharing, where educators had more opportunities to work together, and where there was more teacher voice in decision-making.

Student performance during this study was measured by the California Academic Performance Index, or API, a composite performance measure that reflected students' achievement in a variety of formal assessments.[5] Graduation and dropout rates were also factored into the scores.

We wanted to see whether more collaborative schools in the ABC District experienced greater gains on performance over time. We used the overall API score each school received for the 2011–12 school year, as well as an API *improvement* score based on the overall change in a school's API score from the 2010–11 school year to the 2011–12 school year. We isolated the effect of collaboration by controlling for other key variables, including school type—elementary, middle, or high school—and the level of poverty. Controlling for poverty is particularly important because we know from many other studies that socioeconomic factors have a large impact on student performance.

We found a strong correlation between educator collaboration and student performance by these measures, after controlling for poverty. Here is the headline finding: when comparing among schools on our four-point scale of educator collaboration, each extra point is linked to a 3 percent higher API score, so that the highest set of collaborators in our sample (with a four-point rating) had on average about 9 percent higher API scores than the lowest set (with a one-point rating).[6] In addition, educator collaboration had a very strong relationship to performance improvement within each school: over the course of a year, schools with the highest levels of collaboration sprinted ahead, showing gains as high as 7 percent, while the schools with the lowest levels of collaboration fell further behind, with declines in API as much as 2 percent. Further, partnership and collaboration together explained fully 22 percent of the variation in performance improvement from one year to the next. These findings are all statistically significant.[7]

Figure 2.1 tracks educator collaboration against performance *improvement* for the schools in this study.[8] As the graph illustrates, when the quality of collaboration in a school increases, student performance improves.

Focusing on high-poverty schools, we found that stronger collaboration among administrators and faculty appeared to benefit students from

FIGURE 2.1   Association between educator collaboration and student-achievement gains, controlling for poverty in each school

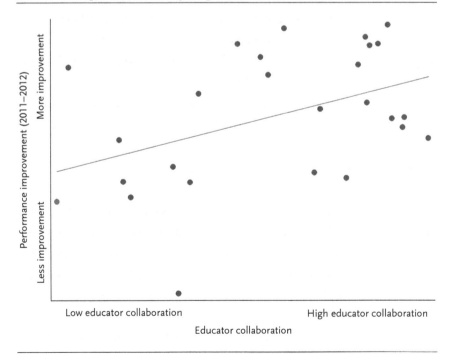

Note: statistically significant: p < .01.

low-income backgrounds as well as those from high-income backgrounds. Student performance was very strongly associated with socioeconomic status; but in both high- and low-poverty schools, collaboration had a positive effect. Indeed, we found in more recent analyses that collaboration has the strongest positive effect in the *least* wealthy schools—despite a small sample the effect was strong enough to be statistically significant. Strong collaboration, in other words, can improve student learning in schools with many disadvantaged students.

The National Survey

Since publishing our research from the ABC Unified School District in California, our team has conducted a larger-scale data collection effort throughout the United States focused on collaborative partnerships and a variety of outcomes for students and educators. We have focused on school and district decision-making and problem-solving, particularly as they apply to the working relationships among administrators, teachers, and their unions. As of this writing, our database includes more than five thousand educators in 450 schools covering twenty-five school districts in six states: California, Illinois, Maine, Massachusetts, Minnesota, and New Jersey.

We are interested in how collaborative processes at the school level impact student performance. As mentioned earlier in this chapter, research on the effects of collaboration on performance can be difficult, as the word *collaboration* is commonly used in a wide range of senses. Being "nice" is not enough.

In the ABC District study described earlier, we were able to dig deeply into the nature of collaboration through interviews, observations, and detailed surveys of the network of social relations across the district. This technique—called social network analysis—allows us to study the relationships between people in an organization using statistics that describe their interaction. In the national study, our evidence extends much more broadly, but less deeply: we know much less about each individual school. Thus, there is more "noise" in the data. We measured collaboration by survey questions about shared decision-making; goal alignment; and teacher discretion, voice, and psychological safety.[9] We also asked about the degree to which teachers view their principals and union leaders as resources.

The key *outcome*—performance—is also hard to assess. Standardized tests are required across the country, but they have been widely criticized as biased, narrow, and inaccurate.[10] Moreover, different states use different tests, so we needed to adjust the reported results to standardize them across states. We also included survey items to measure other important outcomes that contribute to the strength of any education system: high teacher engagement, low teacher turnover, and sharing of innovation.

Despite the limitations of the data in the national sample, the basic pattern observed in the ABC District appears to generalize. After controlling for student poverty and other relevant school characteristics, the more collaborative schools in our sample achieve on average significantly higher levels in the percentage of students who "meet or exceed expectations" on standardized tests for English language arts (ELA) and mathematics.

For the 2015–16 academic year, we were able to match math and ELA performance data to 162 schools surveyed. Figure 2.2 shows school-level collaboration predicting the percentage of students performing at or above standards in ELA, after we controlled for poverty, teacher experience, and school type (elementary, middle, or high school). The mean level of school poverty (measured by the percentage of students receiving free or reduced-price lunch) in the sample was 55 percent, slightly above the national average for that year.[11] In every district, we sought participation from a diverse range of stakeholders, including union presidents, superintendents, school principals, school building union leaders, and K–12 teachers.

Again, the results were positive and statistically significant. For example, on a seven-point scale, a one-point gain in collaboration was associated with another 1.5 percent of students meeting or exceeding expectations on

FIGURE 2.2   Association between collaboration and English language arts achievement scores, controlling for poverty

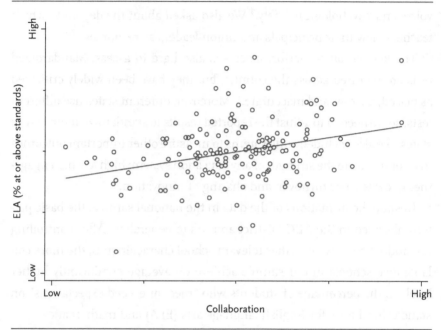

Note: statistically significant: p < .01.

the standardized ELA test (see figure 2.2). The results on the standardized math tests were also statistically significant.

Finally, some of the strongest evidence comes from our New Jersey effort (see part IV of this book). While we have not yet surveyed all of these districts, one superintendent has collected data over time since the Collaborative Partnership was initiated in his district. He summarized the results this way:

> We started out with a challenge and our challenge focused around student achievement. There's been an increase in the national and the New Jersey Student Learning Assessments [standardized test result scores] across

every grade span, and in every subject area, and in all of our at-risk sub-groups. We've had double digit proficiency rate increases, as determined by the [NJ] Department of Education against their learning standards, in every subgroup and in every test area since 2015. Annual student growth has improved and our student attendance has increased. And all of this has been the result of the increase of teacher voice and teacher synergy with leadership within all of our structures, all of our systems. We do believe that collaboration drives achievement.

We are not the first to show the benefits of collaboration for performance. A long tradition of research in other industries reaches the same conclusion; we will review that evidence in chapter 4. In the education sector, there has been less direct research on collaboration as such. But a large meta-study of "comprehensive school reform" efforts, based largely on collaborative principles, found that they had strong performance results and that schools that had implemented the models for five years or more had particularly strong effects.[12] Another pilot study also found significant positive, though moderate, effects of teacher collaboration.[13] An influential study by Frits Pil and Carrie Leana looked at teachers' social capital—defined as frequent interactions between teachers focused on instruction and characterized by feelings of closeness—which is a fair proxy for what we mean by *collaboration*. In a sample of more than one thousand fourth- and fifth-grade teachers at 130 elementary schools across New York City, the authors found that teachers high in social capital increased their students' mathematics scores by 5.7 percent more than teachers with lower social capital scores.[14]

There has been a great deal of research on these intermediate variables—interteacher communication, social capital, and feelings of empowerment—which themselves have been shown to positively affect performance.[15] In addition, there are a large number of studies linking "teacher efficacy" to increased student achievement, and others that link collaboration to teacher efficacy.[16]

Why Do Collaborative Organizations Frequently Outperform?

Collaborative organizations create at least three major advantages for school performance. First, they combine knowledge from multiple contributors with different perspectives on the problem. No single administrator can know as much as a combination of people in different parts of the organization.

Second, collaborative organizations generally increase teachers' learning and professional development. When teachers work isolated from one another and have limited opportunities to participate in decision-making, they may make an impact on student learning through exceptional effort or skill in the classroom, but they will also have to figure things out themselves and learn more slowly, and their innovations will not spread to other teachers. By contrast, in a collaborative environment, teachers learn from one another. They receive assistance, support, ideas, mentoring, and feedback from their peers, while providing colleagues with the same. Interaction makes them better and more resilient teachers.

A third reason that collaborative organizations outperform is that they tend to do a better job of fostering goal alignment, common understanding, and commitment. In traditional bureaucracies, leaders often set new priorities at the top, but they don't have mechanisms to build commitment at the ground level. But in collaborative systems, strategic priorities are constantly discussed at all levels, so that people pull in the same direction. This focused alignment of teacher problem-solving and leadership support produces far stronger and more consistent results than more traditional processes.

An elementary school principal in New Jersey explains the reach, complexity, and importance of this alignment process in his school and across the district:

> Collaborative structures are proven to have enhanced our ability to create
> a positive school climate, build trust among team members, and increase

resources for improvement. That includes human resources, material, technology resources, PTA support, and out-of-district resources such as speakers, authors, organizations, etc.

We've created a system for problem-solving, decision-making and implementation in all areas of our work. We've enhanced communication and information sharing throughout teams and classrooms. Two-way communication is at the forefront. Information from the administrative level and the District Leadership Team is communicated to our School Leadership Team, which in turn is communicated from team leaders to classroom teachers. Likewise, teachers' needs, concerns, and ideas typically travel back up through the same channels. So, with all of this in place, we achieve our ultimate goals of providing effective instruction and a positive school experience for all [the students].

Collaborative Partnerships are problem-focused, using collaboration as a means to find the underlying causes of poor performance and generate solutions to improve teaching and learning. Furthermore, implementation is more effective because educators with deep tacit knowledge who are closest to the problems, and have worked together to solve them, have widespread ownership of the solutions and are the key stakeholders driving the improvement process.

COLLABORATION REDUCES TEACHER TURNOVER

Collaboration also helps with another crucial problem facing public education: teacher shortages and turnover. As discussed in chapter 1, the inability to attract and retain qualified teachers has been identified as a growing problem for some decades, but it reached crisis levels during the COVID-19 pandemic. A 2022 poll conducted by the National Education Association reported that 55 percent of public-school educators planned to leave education sooner than expected due to pandemic-related stress; and the RAND Corporation reported that almost three-fourths of school districts nationwide were experiencing or anticipating shortages of qualified teachers.[17] In 2022, 45 percent of schools reported vacancies in special education jobs, and 31 percent of schools reported vacancies in elementary school jobs.[18] The number of students graduating with education BAs has more than halved in just under fifty years, from over 176,000 in 1971 to 85,000 in 2020.[19]

High teacher turnover is especially prevalent in schools with high poverty levels, where work environments create unique challenges. Relative to students in wealthier communities, poor students are less likely to receive assistance and additional academic support outside of the school. Adversities such as hunger, safety, and violence can contribute to a more destabilized school environment.[20] As a consequence, teachers who serve low-income schools tend to assume greater responsibility for students' academic performance and social and emotional development.

The neoliberal policies described in chapter 1, especially No Child Left Behind, have disproportionately penalized urban schools serving students of color and those living in poverty.[21] Educators teaching students in poorer areas often face the greatest pressure to raise test scores.

Collaboration's Effect on Teacher Turnover and Retention: The Evidence

We have found that turnover in collaborative schools is significantly lower than in less collaborative peers; and for high-poverty schools, the link of collaboration to lower turnover is dramatic.

We explored the effects of collaboration and student poverty on teacher retention across two separate studies. The first of these studies was of the ABC District, where more than 45 percent of the student body were eligible for free or reduced-price lunch.[22] We assessed teacher perceptions of school collaboration annually over four years (2012–15). After averaging these survey questions by school, we paired the values with the voluntary turnover rate for each school over the same period. We found significantly lower voluntary turnover rates in schools with higher levels of collaboration.

Perhaps the most important finding, however, was that the link was particularly strong for high-poverty schools. For these schools—where turnover is a particularly severe ongoing problem—turnover among the more collaborative schools was less than half that of the less collaborative ones.

When collaboration was low, we found that turnover in high-poverty schools was 3.5 times the rate of that in wealthier schools. But when collaboration was high, the voluntary turnover rate in high-poverty schools dropped sharply, even a bit *below* their wealthier peers. We plot this effect in figure 2.3. The level of student poverty is strongly associated with a higher voluntary turnover rate—but only when the collaborative processes

FIGURE 2.3   Effect of interaction of educator collaboration and student poverty on voluntary teacher turnover

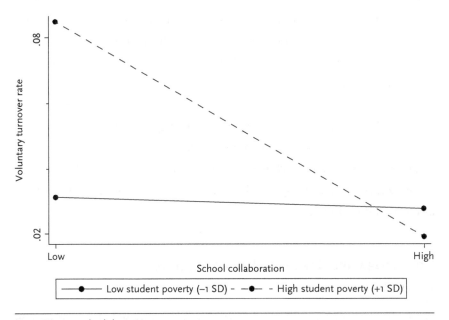

Note: SD = standard deviation.

in the schools are low.[23] The solid line is for wealthier schools: it shows that greater collaboration (moving from left to right) is associated with a decline in teacher turnover. But the dotted line for high-poverty districts shows a really dramatic decline in turnover as collaboration increases. Strong collaboration, in other words, completely negated the difference in teacher turnover between wealthy and low-income schools as there was no statistical difference between teacher turnover in high-poverty and wealthier schools.

We explored similar analyses in our national database, described earlier. We could not measure turnover directly; instead, we measured teachers' self-reported commitment to staying in their current school, which is known to strongly predict actual turnover. The results matched the research from the ABC District: collaborative school cultures corresponded to significantly higher levels of teacher commitment across the board, and the effects were especially strong in schools serving low-income communities. As illustrated in figure 2.4, high student poverty led to lower teacher commitment only when school collaboration was low. However, if collaboration was high, teacher commitment was similar across wealthier and high-poverty schools. Just like turnover in the ABC District, at the highest levels of collaboration, there was no statistical difference between teacher commitment in high-poverty and wealthier schools.

Although they rely on entirely different samples, these two studies show remarkably similar patterns. They also challenge the narrative that high-poverty schools are doomed to endless cycles of teacher attrition.

Figure 2.3 showed a *decline* in turnover with increasing collaboration. Figure 2.4 is a mirror image: it shows a sharp *rise* in teacher commitment as collaboration increases.

COLLABORATIVE SCHOOLS ARE ATTRACTIVE TO TEACHERS

While the study just discussed suggests that collaboration helps retain teachers in their schools, our research also shows that schools where principals

FIGURE 2.4   Effect of interaction of educator collaboration and student poverty on organizational commitment

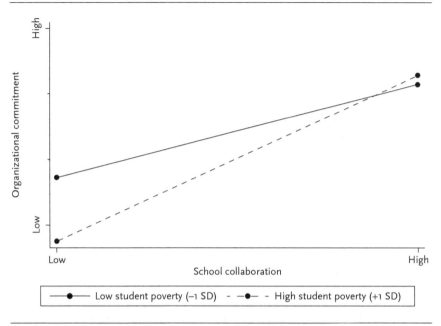

Note: SD = standard deviation.

are seen as collaborative are also likely to benefit by becoming magnets for teachers, with open jobs generating more interest from teachers in other parts of the district. In ninety-two schools across several school districts, we asked teachers to evaluate the degree to which they saw other schools in their district as "attractive places to work." After controlling for a host of variables, including poverty and past performance, teachers rated collaborative schools as much more attractive than less collaborative schools. Teachers judged these schools as more desirable because of the degree to which their colleagues reported having a voice in improving the quality of education at their schools, the degree to which principals solicited their input about student education issues, and whether principals listened to faculty ideas about ways to improve their schools. Teachers received these evaluations from their colleagues through the robust communications networks they develop within school districts.[24]

CONCLUSION

The studies presented in this chapter demonstrate in a variety of ways that educator collaboration can significantly improve student performance. Our work confirms what others have found about the negative impact of poverty on school performance; however, our research also suggests that even in high-poverty schools, student achievement can be significantly improved by increasing educator collaboration, elevating teacher voice, and by sharing planning, problem-solving, and decision-making between administrators, faculty, and staff. Our work also shows that when this happens, turnover drops, schools become more attractive to teachers, and educators become more committed to staying in the profession. This may be part of the solution to the teacher shortage crisis that has grown over the past decades and reached epidemic proportions during the COVID-19 pandemic.

This research clearly shows that collaborative systems have been able to move the needle on student performance, something the neoliberal and bureaucratic reforms of the past forty years have not been able to achieve. Testing alone can only reveal deficiencies in student knowledge, offering little more beyond alerting parents and teachers to a problem. Collaborative systems, because they focus all stakeholders on improving teaching and learning, take the critical next steps and help drive thinking about ways to increase student learning. These systems find solutions to gaps in student achievement and then effectively implement those solutions because educators closest to the problem—with deep knowledge of it—are directly engaged in the improvement process.

CHAPTER 3

Partnership as a Framework for Collaboration

PARTNERSHIP, AS WE HAVE NOTED, is distinct from collaboration. Most cases of collaboration consist only of internal discussions within the existing organizational hierarchy. Partnership brings independent stakeholders into the process, which complicates matters because groups with different power bases have to build a sense of alignment and shared purpose. The evidence in this chapter shows that partnership can significantly increase the benefits of collaboration by extending relations of trust to parties who may otherwise have conflictual relationships.

The US public school system has many important stakeholders, most notably: parents, represented by school boards and (more distantly) by state and local governments; administrators, usually with their own associations; and teachers, school staff, and other employees, some represented by unions. We have involved all of these in our Collaborative Partnership in New Jersey.

One institutional stakeholder, however, has drawn particular attention: the teacher unions. We recognize that not every school system has union representation, that some have unions without collective bargaining power, and that other stakeholder groups are also very important to the mission. We will nevertheless focus here on the issue of labor-management partnership for several reasons. First, there is a long tradition of practice and research around union-management partnerships, which gives us an important base of knowledge and experience. Second, teachers are the most heavily involved every day in the core mission of education. Third, unions often have much larger organizations and greater resources than the associations of other groups, such as school boards and administrators.

In this chapter, we develop evidence that the addition of partnership, especially labor-management partnership, adds to the benefits of collabora-tion detailed in the last chapter. When partnerships are strong, educators throughout the school district are much more likely to move coherently and cooperatively toward a shared vision for school improvement, creating social capital for teachers. And we found that partnerships are a catalyst for collaboration: when school districts have strong union-management partnerships, they are more likely to have higher levels of collaboration in their schools.[1]

Beyond fostering collaborative school cultures, partnerships can strengthen school districts' capacity by drawing on a particular strength of unions: their ability to build effective networks of communication among teachers within and across schools and districts. The networks that emerge within the union infrastructure can, we find, result in more open and innovative schools.

THE BENEFITS OF LABOR-MANAGEMENT PARTNERSHIPS IN EDUCATION

Our research described earlier, from the ABC Unified School District of California and in a separate sample of 450 schools across six states, showed evidence that effective union-management partnerships strengthen collaborative systems and therefore lead to greater improvements in stu-dent performance than are seen in schools with weaker partnerships. We have also identified some of the mechanisms by which that improvement happens:

1. Where partnerships are strong, union leaders become conduits of knowledge and innovation, building networks of relationships across schools and districts that bring understanding of effective educational methods to more teachers.

2. Partnerships also lead to increases in the social capital of teachers themselves—that is, the scope of their relationships of trust and sharing around issues of teaching and learning.

Partnership Districts Foster More Collaborative Schools

Chapter 2 established the link between collaboration and student performance. However, just as important, we have also found that partnerships are a significant predictor of collaboration. Strong union-management partnerships provide a context that favors internal collaboration and therefore student performance.

Strong evidence for this dynamic is detailed in our 2016 article in *ILR Review*, based on the detailed study of the ABC District described in chapter 2. We used surveys and interviews to measure the strength of the union-management partnership—especially how often the leaders of the two institutions communicated. We also measured the strength of collaboration through questions about how the school plans and initiatives were developed. Finally, we used the standardized test results from California as our outcome measure of student achievement.

In these studies, we found a chain of statistically significant relations:

Union-management partnership → educator collaboration → student achievement

This may be a surprising finding for some. While a number of scholars have suggested that the presence of unions is associated with improved organizational performance,[2] others have argued the opposite.[3] But actual research has been sparse. Although there are many studies of union-management partnership in other industries, there are few extensive ones in public schools.[4] Further, there has been little exploration of the causal mechanisms by which labor-management partnerships affect student performance. While several studies have shown that greater levels of social capital and collaboration can have positive implications for student performance, little is known about the institutional antecedents to collaboration.[5]

We fill this void in the literature by establishing an empirical connection between union-management partnerships and student performance. Moreover, our research is unique in demonstrating *reasons* that such partnerships can have a positive effect and the conditions under which they are most effective. Union-management partnerships, we find, serve as catalysts for collaboration in public schools by creating a culture that elevates the voice of teachers as professionals and an infrastructure for shared problem-solving and decision-making with management. These findings defy the narrative that unions are necessarily barriers to innovation and change.[6]

We also examined in the ABC District the relationship between the quality of the school union-management partnership and the *density of collaboration* between educators in the building. We found that partnership quality was associated with educator communication on four topics: (1) student performance data, (2) curriculum development, (3) mentoring, and (4) sharing instructional practices or pedagogy. The pattern was the same across all four topics, so we combined them in the bar chart shown in figure 3.1 to illustrate the relationship between partnership and collaboration. As we can see in the figure, the schools with the strongest partnerships had almost twice the communication density (30 percent) of schools with the weakest partnerships (17 percent). On average, 30 percent of the educators in the strongest partnership schools had at least weekly communications with one another about student performance, curriculum development, mentoring, or instructional practice, while in the weak partnership schools, only 17 percent of educators collaborated weekly on one or more of those topics. Strong partnership schools are characterized by much more widespread collaboration.[7]

We also looked specifically at the relationship between partnership quality and the collaboration between school-building union leaders and principals.

FIGURE 3.1 School communications density: percentage of teachers with regular communication ties to one another

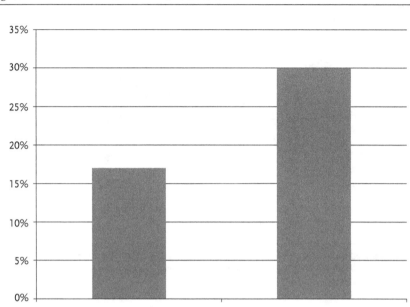

Source: Based on Saul A. Rubinstein and John E. McCarthy, *Teachers Unions and Management Partnerships: How Working Together Improves Student Achievement* (Washington, DC: Center for American Progress, 2014).

We found that the stronger the partnership quality, the greater the probability that union leaders and their principals had frequent communication. Further, in strong partnership schools, the communication was more informal than in schools with weaker partnerships. Figures 3.2 and 3.3 illustrate this point. Figure 3.2 shows that in strong partnership schools, communication occurred daily and weekly between union leaders and principals, while weak partnership schools were characterized by communications between union leaders and principals that occurred mostly weekly or monthly.

Figure 3.3 shows that in strong partnership schools, those more frequent communications between union leaders and principals were both formal and informal, occurring in one another's offices or the cafeteria or hallways,

FIGURE 3.2 Communication frequencies between principals and union school building representatives by strong and weak partnership schools*

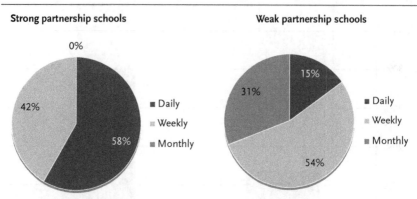

* Strong partnership schools fell in the top half for partnership quality; weak partnership fell in the bottom half

Source: Based on Saul A. Rubinstein and John E. McCarthy, *Teachers Unions and Management Partnerships: How Working Together Improves Student Achievement* (Washington, DC: Center for American Progress, 2014).

FIGURE 3.3 Communication formality between principals and union school building representatives by strong and weak partnership schools*

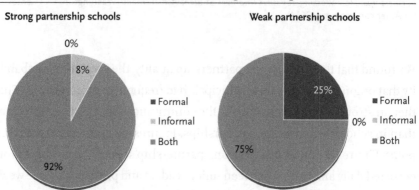

* Strong partnership schools fell in the top half for partnership quality; weak partnership fell in the bottom half

Source: Based on Saul A. Rubinstein and John E. McCarthy, *Teachers Unions and Management Partnerships: How Working Together Improves Student Achievement* (Washington, DC: Center for American Progress, 2014).

while in weak partnership schools, the less frequent communication was more formal through scheduled events such as faculty meetings. We conclude that there are structural differences between the union-management collaboration in stronger-partnership schools when compared to weaker-partnership schools.[8]

Unions Build Learning Networks Across Schools and Districts

Another important effect of union-management partnerships is that union leaders, when partnerships are strong, build networks of relationships across schools and districts that link their members—teachers and staff—to new ranges of trusted knowledge and innovation.

In research published in 2019, we studied the boundary-spanning activities of school site union leaders.[9] We found that they play an important role in the dissemination of knowledge and innovative practices from across the school district, thus contributing to the improvement of teaching and learning.

Boundary spanners are individuals whose social networks reach beyond the boundaries of their work group or function. These external networks are especially valuable as work becomes increasingly complex, and knowledge-based organizations need boundary spanners to facilitate the exchange of information, ideas, and resources throughout the organization. Through these external networks, boundary spanners are able to give their work groups access to external knowledge, perspectives, and practices that they can adapt to improve their own units.[10] Within organizations, research has demonstrated the link between the presence of boundary-spanning networks and team performance.[11]

Schools, too, need boundary spanners. Like any kind of organization, schools can become tied to a narrow set of perspectives and assumptions, which often limit their potential for meaningful change. Scholars thus argue for the importance of looking beyond the school building for sources of change and performance improvement. Stoll and Seashore-Louis write that "without due attention to fostering ties outside the school, strong professional communities can, paradoxically, become a barrier to change."[12]

Hargreaves and Giles emphasize that school districts must bring "together the knowledge, skills and dispositions of teachers in a school or across schools to promote shared learning and improvement."[13]

School districts therefore benefit from knowledge-sharing networks that extend beyond school buildings, enabling access to external knowledge and other resources.[14] The practices and learning techniques acquired at other schools become the foundation for meaningful innovation and professional improvement.[15]

We have found that union leaders have communication networks that extend beyond the school building and beyond departments or grade levels within the school building. We have explored how boundary-spanning union leaders communicate and collaborate with teachers and union leaders in other schools, with administrators at the district and school level, and with their own principals to access and disseminate knowledge and innovative practices in their schools and throughout the district.

How Boundary Spanners Spread Knowledge and Innovation

Our 2019 study documented this role of union leaders in the ABC District.[16] Through qualitative and quantitative network analyses, we found strong links between the number of school union leaders' boundary-spanning ties and teachers' use of knowledge from other schools.

As described in chapter 2, the ABC District developed a strong union-management partnership over several decades. In a social network analysis that studied the communication patterns of leaders across the district, every school-level union leader reported having professional communications with other union colleagues outside their school. When we mapped patterns of exchange through a detailed study of the district as a communications network, we could isolate the central role of union representatives, especially in extending communication beyond the school walls. The analysis also showed that teachers had a more positive view of union leaders who had active networks: they saw them as greater *resources* to access information on classroom instructional practices and other school-improvement-related opportunities outside of their schools. In our national study, we had a parallel finding—that teachers in highly collaborative schools saw their union representative as a greater resource. These teachers also reported that they found their principal to be a greater resource than did teachers in less collaborative schools.

We have found from interviews and observations that one of the reasons that this network works so well is that exchanges with peers—which the union helps to mediate—are more trusted and seen as more useful than materials sent down through the official hierarchy.

One year after this exploratory social network analysis, we surveyed the district's school union leaders and teachers. We also measured the extent of union leaders' networks through another social network survey administered to all union leaders from every school in the district. Respondents were asked to identify individuals with whom they shared professional, work-related communications—particularly task-oriented interactions. We also asked these union leaders to indicate others outside of their school with whom they "communicate to share, advise, or learn about instructional practices." The average union leader held connections to approximately seven other schools in the district.

Then we measured the outcome: the extent of teacher learning acquired through the union leader network. In the districtwide survey administered to all teachers in the district, we asked teachers their degree of agreement with two statements: (1) "I am up to date with the instructional strategies being used by other schools in the district," and (2) "I draw from what other schools in the district are doing to get better."

The data showed that in schools that were highly collaborative and where union leader boundary-spanners have better external connections, teachers are 50 percent more likely to receive and use knowledge of instructional practices from other schools. We found the positive effect of union leaders' networks to be virtually nonexistent in less collaborative schools where principals discouraged employee voice and participation in planning, problem-solving, and decision-making.

Who Are the Best Boundary Spanners?

Studies have shown that formal leaders, including supervisors or managers, are often the most effective boundary spanners.[17] This is not surprising; formal leaders have more opportunities to build and maintain relationships outside of their immediate work group.[18] The higher your position in the organizational hierarchy, the more extensive your social network. Boundary spanning is also difficult and time-intensive.[19] Managers often have more opportunities to build and maintain diverse relationships than frontline employees. Conferences, meetings, and informal social gatherings offer leaders opportunities to build horizontal connections with other managers and vertical connections to upper management.[20] The same dynamic holds true in the context of schools: the social networks of administrators, unlike those of most teachers, reach across the district.[21]

However, our research showed that the *most* effective boundary-spanning networks in schools belong to local union leaders. Our studies of the ABC District found that only union leaders' networks predicted innovation sharing; our study of the network of principals did not show a relationship to sharing of knowledge across schools. Figure 3.4 is a netgraph—a visualization of the network of educators in one middle school building in the ABC District. It also shows the network of principals and the network of building union leaders.

Why are union leaders particularly effective as boundary spanners? Their networks include union leaders in other schools in the district and in other districts. Like principals, union representatives have abundant opportunities to build and maintain professionally productive relationships outside of their school. But most important, they have relatively strong and trusting relations with the teachers who have elected them and therefore are more effective in transferring information, knowledge, and resources.[22]

Other teachers can, of course, develop relations across schools, fostered at professional development meetings or through school transfers, but these are likely to be more sporadic. Union leaders, on the other hand, are

FIGURE 3.4 Networks of building union leaders and principals

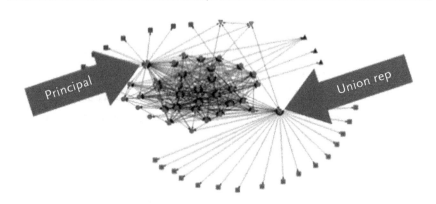

connected through regular institutional mechanisms to wider networks that not only help to foster relationships but also keep them active and productive.

Significantly, these findings further reinforce the importance of partnership: they suggest that the benefits of union leaders' boundary-spanning activities depend heavily on the willingness of administrators to work with them. School principals can be gatekeepers to collaboration; whether union leaders can successfully leverage their networks for the benefit of their schools and the school districts is partly in the hands of these principals.

Our research emphasizes two characteristics of successful boundary spanners. First, they must be connected to other leaders who have resources to offer. Second, for individuals' social networks to be effective, they must be influential within their schools. Dissemination rests on the individuals' collaboration with their colleagues in their schools.

The Contribution of the Institutional Partnership

It is not just individual union leaders who build learning networks: we have evidence that the *unions as institutions*, when involved in ongoing partnerships, can further organize and magnify that effect. In another longitudinal study, we showed that the strengthening of partnership—improved relations and greater communication between administration and union leadership—caused union leaders' interaction networks to expand further, including networks focused on improvement in teaching and learning. Again, because these data are longitudinal, we can state this causally: the strengthening of Collaborative Partnerships over time causes increased engagement of school union leaders in diverse improvement-oriented initiatives within and between schools.[23]

Union Leaders' Contributions to Managerial Decisions

Union leaders bring a distinctive perspective to managerial decision-making: they have to be elected by their members. Thus their focus tends to be on preserving the long-run stability of the company. Management leaders, especially at the top, are driven primarily by the needs of shareholders, which leads to different priorities.

Neither the management nor the union perspective is "right" for all people all the time. There have been occasions in which unions, focused on member demands, have resisted needed change and undermined company competitiveness, ultimately harming their members. But there have also been occasions in which the managerial focus on shareholder value has led to excessive focus on short-term returns, with destructive results. The larger point is that the process of engaging in joint decision-making is more likely to result in decisions that balance these perspectives and create a sounder basis for long-term development.

Because of the independence of unions, their leaders can question positions or decisions taken by management. Because they are protected by collective bargaining agreements, they are freer than their non-represented counterparts to express independent judgment and disagree with upper management without fear of reprisal. In addition, the typical career paths of union leaders don't take them to other companies, unlike their counterparts in management. As a result, union leaders consider the long-term success of their current organization or school as essential to their own individual futures.

For all these reasons, unions can offer alternative perspectives to supplement the perspectives of non-represented management. Arriving with different perspectives doesn't mean automatic conflict. These perspectives enrich the decision-making process—and, as a bonus, are more likely to encourage employees, who were allowed to offer their viewpoints, to support the final decision.

Thus, by designing and administering collaborative initiatives in an organization, unions are not only adding value to the firm: they are helping create systems that can potentially outperform nonunion forms of participation.

Partnership Improves Teachers' Job Satisfaction and Social Capital

Further benefits flow from collaborative labor-management partnerships. First, they lead to an improvement in the job satisfaction of teachers. In a survey of 513 educators from two school districts comprising sixty-one schools, we found that labor-management partnership by itself is strongly associated with higher job satisfaction of teachers; it creates a positive atmosphere in the workplace. And the interaction with the network of union leader boundary-spanners adds to this effect, further improving job satisfaction.[24]

In a new analysis for this book, we found that labor-management partnership also contributes to teachers' social capital. We collected data on the climate and culture of five districts at the start of their partnership-building efforts and again multiple times over the ensuing years. Thus, we could then examine how changes in partnership quality changed aspects of collaborative culture over time.

In each district, we surveyed union presidents and superintendents about the quality, regularity, and content of interactions throughout the school district. Teachers in high partnership school districts reported having more access to positive relationships across their school districts—that is, teachers in high partnership districts were much more likely to report that their colleagues were trustworthy, openly shared information, and were committed to advancing the same goals. Because this study is longitudinal, it provides especially strong evidence of causation—in other words, that Collaborative Partnership causes the strengthening of teachers' relations focused on teaching and learning.

Finally, in addition to supporting innovation and improvement, the social networks of union boundary spanners can assist their members in other ways, such as helping to steer organizational resources to members or keeping them aware of opportunities in more attractive collaborative schools in other parts of the district.[25] We will discuss this finding further in chapter 6.

Other Benefits

Surveys don't tell us everything: they are necessarily focused on narrow questions. We have learned a good deal through observation and experiences that further fill out the picture.

Organizational networks are increasingly important when change is rapid and flexibility, responsiveness, and problem-solving are critical for success. Institutional partnerships facilitate the creation of such networks, linking people across organizations who have the knowledge and resources necessary for rapid coordination, effective decision-making, and problem-solving. When partners use their infrastructure to help create these networks, high levels of trust can result, and this adds tremendous value to organizational innovation, responsiveness, and effectiveness.[26]

A major benefit has been the reduction in conflict, which saps organizational energy and often impedes progress. Research on labor-management partnerships has long proposed that unions can improve organizational and employee outcomes by taking ownership of professional issues beyond traditional bargaining and grievances.[27] We have observed this in the New Jersey Public School Collaborative. A local union president in New Jersey said:

> Collaboration does not mean we always agree. . . . We have chosen to sit at the same table, to plan together, where all voices are heard, rather than file grievances after decisions are made. Speaking of grievances, I can't remember the last time we actually filed a grievance in this school district. It's a testament to our structure and our commitment to work together at all levels.

Thus, in effective partnerships, change is often far smoother and more effective than usual. Management receives more suggestions, ideas, information, and feedback, and unions are able to influence changes. In these processes, the partners are working together to improve teaching and learning.

We saw this most clearly during the COVID-19 pandemic in New Jersey. The districts participating in the Collaborative handled the difficult issues of remote learning, changing schedules, new technology, safety, and other challenges far more smoothly than most other districts. Administrators and teachers worked out innovative ways to maintain the quality of education while lowering the stress. There were no instances of major conflict or strikes, as in other districts in the state. We will elaborate on these experiences during the pandemic in chapter 9.

OTHER PARTNERS

Again, unions are only one partner in the multi-stakeholder education system. We have not conducted the same systematic surveys of other partners—a gap we will need to remedy in the future. But we do have a considerable amount of observational data and experience about their roles, which has been crucial to the successful development of collaborative systems.

This is especially true of the New Jersey case, which we will elaborate in part IV of this book, because it is exceptional in deliberately involving other institutional stakeholders from the beginning. The New Jersey Public School Collaborative began with a support group of leaders from the state associations of school boards, principals and supervisors, and superintendents—along with the two major education unions.

These parties have made substantial contributions to the Collaborative.

1. They have been crucial in helping to recruit new districts, especially in the early years. They actively persuaded their members—who often knew nothing about collaboration and were suspicious of new programs and burdens—that this was something worthwhile.
2. They have helped their members through periods of difficulty and doubt. They have often traveled to the districts of the Collaborative to talk to their counterparts, problem-solve, and build new relationships.
3. They have helped with relations with government officials and regulators. All of these associations have their own connections to various government officials.
4. They have developed education for their members on the working of collaborative systems and their benefits and have reduced the emphasis on adversarial preparation for conflict that has historically characterized many of their training programs—thus helping to shift the culture of the system as a whole.

Here are the perspectives of the three partner associations *other* than the unions:

TIMOTHY PURNELL, EXECUTIVE DIRECTOR/CEO,
NEW JERSEY SCHOOL BOARDS ASSOCIATION:
The concept of collaboration is one we teach even to the youngest students: work together and you can achieve more. The research shows that in school districts where management and unions successfully work together, both student achievement and teacher retention improve. Working together

and building mutual respect can be hard. But the ultimate beneficiaries are our students—and building an educational system where all children can achieve their full potential is the common goal of us all.

VINCENT DE LUCIA, EDUCATOR IN RESIDENCE,
NEW JERSEY SCHOOL BOARDS ASSOCIATION:
All six thousand [School Board] members here in this state would benefit from this process. Some of those things we talk about are climate, culture, equity, social-emotional learning, relationships, and achievement for all kids and adults. That really is the foundation of the work that is happening here.[28]

KAREN BINGERT, EXECUTIVE DIRECTOR,
NEW JERSEY PRINCIPALS AND SUPERVISORS ASSOCIATION:
It takes a village, and the village likes to talk. Part of the benefit of the Collaborative is recognizing that it is the investment of everyone in the space to accomplish what needs to be done. When it comes to the talking part of it, talk can be really negative and undermine a goal, or you can channel that energy so that the village is actually getting something accomplished. If you're all in the same rowboat, no one will let it sink.[29]

DEBRA BRADLEY, DIRECTOR OF GOVERNMENT RELATIONS,
NEW JERSEY PRINCIPALS AND SUPERVISORS ASSOCIATION:
We had some members who were open to it, other members who asked, "Does this make sense for me?" And what we have found is that very experienced members who've been in the profession for years have found that this has strengthened their practice. Brand new principals who have just gotten on the job have also found how this has really helped define their roles and given them credibility with their staff. And all of this was something that they were willing to embrace because the statewide organization was part of the project and willing to support it through every step of the way. So I think working with our other groups, we've all been able to be a bridge to our own memberships.

MARK STANWOOD, DIRECTOR OF RESIDENCY PROGRAM FOR
NEW SUPERINTENDENTS, NEW JERSEY ASSOCIATION OF SCHOOL
ADMINISTRATORS (SUPERINTENDENTS ASSOCIATION):
We participate because we get better decisions with people who have the
experience and perspective that those of us with titles might not have. The
titles of superintendent, assistant superintendent, directors, principals—
those folks with ranks and titles—can't make the quality of decisions that
we can when we ask others who are close to the challenges at hand.[30]

Our work is getting more complex, our challenges more complex,
and complex problems require complex solutions. So we need a lot of
folks around those challenges to understand them better, to rely on their
perspective. And that's why we have embraced this work and are thrilled
to be part of it.

We feel so strongly about collaboration that we make it a [regular] part
of our Academy for New Superintendents, where they hear from [Rutgers]
and practicing superintendents from our districts every year. So it's a
high leverage opportunity that we've discovered because the solutions are
owned and designed by people who are close to the problem.

CONCLUSION: THE SYNERGY OF PARTNERSHIP AND COLLABORATION

To return to our core argument: our evidence shows that partnership and
collaboration form a stronger system than either one alone. Education, like
all industries, engages multiple stakeholders with differing viewpoints and
interests, organized as separate organizations pursuing different missions.
Collaboration within any one of those organizations can make it more
effective, but it doesn't strengthen the system as a whole. Bringing the
stakeholders together as partners creates a synergy across perspectives that
both reduces conflict and combines knowledge in a constructive pursuit
of innovation.

Thus we find, in our particular research projects and in our broader
experience, that there are positive synergies in a system of Collaborative

Partnership. Our research showed, for example, that union leaders in strong partnerships foster learning and innovation in classrooms by building wide networks of peer communication—but this effect is stronger when it is combined with strong collaboration among educators within schools. We also saw that the deepening of partnership itself strengthens collaboration. These improvements in turn led to better school climate, more teacher job satisfaction, lower turnover, and higher student achievement. And as the parties see these results, they become more committed to the system. We see, in short, the evolution of a virtuous circle of change.

PART III

Lessons from the Past

T HIS SECTION DOUBLES BACK to examine the history of collaboration and partnership. The collaborative reform efforts in New Jersey that will be the focus of part IV did not emerge out of thin air: there have been efforts of this type for more than a century, and they have taught us many important lessons.

We have been particularly influenced by traditions of union-management partnership going back to the 1920s and by more recent developments of participatory systems within corporations and other organizations over the past forty years. We have ourselves been engaged in a number of these efforts, including labor-management Quality of Work Life programs in the auto and telecommunications industries; Labor-Management Participation Teams in the steel industry; Quality Circles; self-directed work teams and task forces; strategic dialogues; mutual-gains negotiations; and other innovations in both unionized and nonunion settings.

In this section, we summarize these historical experiments—first looking at efforts in a broad swath of industries, then focusing on efforts in public schools. We will draw on these experiences in the model of Collaborative Partnership described in part IV.

CHAPTER 4

From Taylorist Bureaucracy to Collaborative Systems in Industry

THE STORY OF EDUCATIONAL policy in recent decades, as described in the first chapter—the strange convergence of Democrats and Republicans on a centrally mandated, high-stakes testing regime combined with support for market-driven competition from decentralized charter schools and vouchers—can be understood as part of broader tensions between centralization and decentralization of organizations across many industries.

The mid-twentieth century was the era of centralized bureaucracy—not just in schools, but throughout society.[1] Henry Ford and Frederick Taylor developed the assembly line in 1913; Alfred Sloan deployed the full panoply of layered hierarchy at General Motors in the interwar years; and the federal government grew a wide-ranging set of bureaucratic agencies starting with the New Deal.

The logic of these organizations was simple: each job was clearly defined, and higher levels set the tasks, because they were the only ones who were in a position to understand the system below them and to make fully informed decisions. Managers were rewarded for their ability to solve problems and maintain accountability. Lower levels were expected to dutifully carry out the orders from above.

These organizations dominated the decades after World War II. As late as the 1970s, bureaucracy in both industry and government was generally seen as a good thing: it connoted efficiency, quality, clarity of expectations, and security of employment.

This consensus began to weaken in the 1960s, first because of a growing concern with worker commitment. Experiments began to percolate bringing workers into groups to discuss the quality of their products and their work life and to suggest improvements. This caused a certain amount of tension and confusion because supervisors were no longer confident of their authority. These very limited efforts hardly changed the overall structure.

The system was shaken more profoundly by the growing economic instability of the 1970s, and particularly the globalizing wave of the 1980s. Businesses began to preach a doctrine of flexibility, decentralization, and innovation, of getting "close to the customer" by continuously improving quality. Frontline workers began to be seen as a productive source of new ideas, a competitive advantage rather than simply a cost. The very stability of bureaucracy became a liability; quite quickly, the term became a synonym for unresponsiveness and lack of innovation.

The history of business organizations since then has been one of great experimentation and invention. Some companies have tried radical decentralization—"turning the organization upside down," in consultant-speak; others developed more coordinated systems of teamwork. But it has been a very slow and unsteady process. The habits of bureaucracy run deep: managers want to manage, while many workers just want clarity. And it has been difficult to figure out how to encourage innovation and flexibility without losing consistency and quality. Some industries, especially newer ones such as high tech, now use flexible teams as a core part of normal operations; others are still quite hierarchical.

Government has been much slower to move than industry. There is less competitive pressure and less feedback from end users. Consistency is a higher priority than in the business world. Thus, the many efforts to "debureaucratize" government have had very little success so far.

THE EVOLUTION OF COLLABORATIVE WORK SYSTEMS IN INDUSTRY

We use the term *collaborative* to refer to work systems that involve a significant degree of participative problem-solving and decision-making, rather than bureaucracy's single point of managerial decision-making and one-way control.

Much research on collaborative systems was done during the 1980s and '90s in traditional manufacturing industries, particularly automobiles and steel. These exemplars of bureaucracy, which had been at the core of the economy for decades, were rather abruptly faced with sophisticated and flexible high-quality competitors from other countries.

Japan was a major focus during that period, as Toyota and Honda took huge chunks of the US market. Japanese auto companies involved their workers much more in shop floor decisions and problem-solving. Their system of *kaizen*, or continuous improvement, engaged workers in a continual search for new ideas to eliminate waste, reduce cost, and improve quality. It quickly became apparent that they achieved higher quality and more rapid innovation; American auto companies quickly fell behind. It took well over a decade before US firms made the transition to shop floor "quality improvement teams" as a normal operational method.[2]

These approaches—under names such as *lean production* and *high-performance work systems*—spread rapidly to other manufacturing industries. There was no single model, but there were some general tendencies: vertically, employees were more involved in problem-solving and decisions once reserved for their managers; horizontally, employees received increased training, had greater flexibility on which tasks to perform and how, and engaged in more teamwork on the job. In addition to de-escalating the adversarial relations between labor and management, increased worker involvement in managerial decisions also helped companies reduce the layers of management—fewer supervisors were needed—at a time when American business was recognizing the benefits of "flatter" organizations.

For the most part, however, these efforts remained extremely limited in scope. Since the turn of the century, workplaces focused on knowledge production and management have gone considerably farther, adopting a more radical model centered on the use of flexible, task-focused teams. In the management ranks of IBM, AT&T, Citibank, Lucent, and others where we have conducted research, employees typically work on multiple team projects at once and see their "bosses" only occasionally.[3] The COVID-19 pandemic accelerated this trend. Employees in many companies—at least above the frontline level—have a great deal of discretion about how to organize their work, and they are rewarded for initiative and innovation.[4]

An early example was the turn toward the internet by IBM in the 1990s. At the time, IBM was still an old-line bureaucracy built around making and selling large-scale proprietary computers. The appearance of small personal computers was ignored because it was simply outside the mindset of the organization. A few middle managers, however, struck by the power of this new model, put together a task force on their own initiative. They built alliances across the company, tried some experiments, and gradually built understanding and support for an open internet strategy.[5] Later, a small cross-functional team was sent offsite to develop the first large-selling personal computer.

This case demonstrated the power of shifting out of the bureaucratic culture. It also demonstrated the level of resistance to it from existing management, who never fully embraced the personal computer despite its initial market success.

Over the past few decades, fluid task forces have gone well beyond this marginal or experimental stage and have become an ordinary way of operating in many companies. They are increasingly essential to effective knowledge work because they enable people with different kinds of expertise and experience to combine their knowledge in new ways.[6] Organizations stuck in bureaucratic structures that divide people into narrow jobs and functions are unable to deal with the explosive growth of information and expertise required for any important effort.

A major review of workplace innovation, published by one of the authors and his colleagues, showed that systematic transformations of work practices can lead to high productivity and quality that benefit firms substantially.[7] Other research has shown that this emerging type of organization is especially effective in industries that require a variety in products or services, are technology-dependent, or depend on worker knowledge, quality, innovation, and agility in responding to changes in consumer preferences.[8]

Decisions made collaboratively have been shown to have several advantages. We summarized them for educational institutions in chapter 2, but they apply more broadly. To recap: collaboration combines relevant knowledge and perspectives around complex tasks; it builds understanding and support among those who will be needed to carry out the decision; and it produces broad alignment around shared goals.

In collaborative systems, the enormous quantity of discretionary decisions in every organization—independent judgments constantly being made on the fly—are much more likely to flow in an aligned, consistent direction rather than at cross-purposes.[9] Managers who engage in collaborative processes frequently note that although the decision may take longer when many are involved, the implementation is much smoother and more effective when everyone is on board.[10]

These benefits are seen especially in situations where increased employee knowledge and engagement can make real contributions to organizational performance. This is most true in knowledge-intensive work, though assembly lines have also been shown to operate much more effectively when workers share in decision-making.

In our recent research on union-management partnerships around educator collaboration, we have seen each of these effects replicated or echoed. Teachers align around shared goals; school- and district-level union and administrative leaders make more informed decisions; teachers increasingly bring their voices into key decision-making processes; and communication among teachers and between teachers and administration greatly increases.

At the same time, it is clear that collaborative efforts—particularly *transitions* from bureaucratic structures and habits—are difficult: they require sustained leadership attention and support. They almost always spark resistance from managers and entrenched actors at all levels. Some of this resistance is simply driven by narrow defensiveness, but some makes more sense from an organizational perspective: rapid organization change can be very disruptive, and performance can be harmed in the short run by confusion about new roles, processes, and expectations. Thus, many collaborative efforts fail; others do well for a time but fall back into old modes when leadership changes.

UNION-MANAGEMENT PARTNERSHIPS

The Early History: Partnership Without Collaboration

There is a long history in the US private sector of joint union-management partnerships to improve organizational performance, gaining momentum during the 1920s in the textile, apparel, and railway industries.[11] The discussion of how unions can add value to the firm has gone through several phases. The traditional view of business unionism saw the role of organized labor as bargaining contracts and protecting worker rights under those contracts to ensure fair and humane treatment. For early twentieth-century advocates of business unionism, this social value of "industrial jurisprudence"—protecting worker rights through a system of rules—was the extent of the unions' mandates. Management, these early unionists believed, should be left to managers. To become involved in management, they believed, would destroy the independence of the union that was required for unions to challenge management decisions.

In the 1920s and 1930s, however, unions in some industries began widespread efforts to add value to their firms through increased involvement in planning, problem-solving, and decision-making.[12] Sumner Slichter concluded that these partnership arrangements could resolve contradictions between industrial jurisprudence, which protects worker rights through a system of rules, and the productivity that can be restricted by those rules. In most of these early experiments with participation in managerial decision-making—such as those in the steel and automobile industries from the 1920s to the 1940s—frontline workers did not actively participate in decisions. Unions were involved largely in off-line representative forms of participation: that is, top-level union leaders had a say in decisions that did not involve day-to-day operations. The International Ladies Garment Workers Union (ILG) and the Amalgamated Clothing Workers (ACW) engaged in systems of union-management cooperation to add value to company performance, while still pursuing their mandate to organize and protect workers' rights under collective bargaining. However, the ILG and ACW initiatives were undermined to some extent by their top-level approach to collaboration. While full-time union leaders might be working with management, the rank and file continued to have no voice in decisions related to their day-to-day work.

Partnership efforts in the railroad industries, particularly in the shop crafts, were stronger during this time period because, unlike in the textile and apparel industries, the International Association of Machinists (IAM) union and railroad management created shop-level joint labor-management committees. These committees contributed to overall business performance by focusing on waste reduction as well as working conditions. The Baltimore and Ohio Cooperation Plan, for example, began in 1923 and was successful for many years, leading to improved productivity, quality, and labor relations. The devastation of the Great Depression put an end to many of these early efforts at union-management cooperation, but a precedent for productive collaboration had been set.

These efforts expanded during the organizing drives after the New Deal and were extensive in the armaments industries during the early and mid-1940s.[13] During World War II, the production demands put on industry by the war encouraged leaders of the United Auto Workers, United Steel-workers, and United Electrical Workers, as well as the IAM, to launch a new phase of union-management partnership in an effort to increase productivity. More than six hundred plant-level labor-management committees were established in industries supporting the war effort, leading to increased product quantity and quality. Once again, the structure for union-management partnership limited participation to union leaders, not the rank and file. In addition, the labor-management committees were organized off–line—that is, they were structures that existed outside of the normal production or managerial activities.

As the war ended and wartime production demands dissipated, so too, did attraction companies might have developed for union-management partnership. United Auto Workers (UAW) President Walter Reuther tried to revive the momentum through collective bargaining proposals to General Motors (GM) in 1945 and 1948 in which the union offered to tie wage increases to prices but required that GM open its books to the union. GM declined. By the 1950s, wartime union-management arrangements had all but disappeared, and management reasserted its claim to managerial prerogatives. They believed if unions did contribute to firm performance, this contribution was an incidental outcome of unions' focus on wage bargaining: for example, higher wages might motivate managers to seek higher productivity.

There have been some notable examples of union-management partnership in Europe. In some industries, unions have almost half of the seats on boards of directors, under European Union statutes requiring "co-determination." On occasion, American unions have also gained board seats, usually in companies in crisis, such as Eastern Airlines after 1984 and several steel companies in the 1990s. Much more common are arrangements in which union leaders get some say in some decisions for which their support is particularly needed. When they work well, such systems maintain labor peace, but they are far from engaging the full capabilities of the workforce.

Partnership Plus Collaboration

Those early efforts were in effect partnerships without collaboration: that is, management and union officials shared some power at high levels, but the basic work continued to be fragmented and bureaucratically managed. However, as we saw earlier, during this period pressures on managers were growing to engage workers more deeply at the workplace. The restrictions placed on worker voice by the mass production systems of Scientific Management, which separated thinking (management's work) from doing (labor's work), were both oppressive and inefficient.

Thus cases began to appear of what we call Collaborative Partnership, in which committees of union and management leaders coordinated direct involvement of rank-and-file workers in decision-making. The "Quality of Work Life" movement of the 1970s and '80s established worker teams under the auspices of joint union-management committees; it spread through the auto and steel industries and achieved a large scope at AT&T. A few cases went deeper: union and the management worked together at all levels, and many decisions were made in a collaborative manner. In the steel, pharmaceutical, glass, defense, and auto industries, partnerships provided for direct member participation in daily operational decisions through on-line self-directed work teams.[14]

Finally, a few local unions in the auto and steel industries developed multiple forms of participation that reinforced one another: direct participation involving the rank-and-file, representative participation through union leadership, and decision-making related to both off-line and on-line processes. These cases included the Harman auto mirror plant in Bolivar, Tennessee, and the Shell refinery in Sarnia, Canada.[15]

Probably the most developed example of Collaborative Partnership in industry was the Saturn Corporation—a subsidiary of General Motors—an experiment ahead of its time and facing opposition from entrenched forces in both the UAW and GM, while also showing the potential of this combination.[16]

THE SATURN CASE: A REVOLUTION IN
INDUSTRIAL CO-MANAGEMENT

Structures for Expanded Employee Participation

In the early 1980s, General Motors concluded it was unable to compete with Japanese automakers on cost and quality in the small-car market; so it embarked on a joint venture with the UAW to design and build a small car in the United States. Both the design of the car and the design of the organization and production system were to be innovative and state-of-the-art. GM even adopted the slogan "A Different Kind of Company, A Different Kind of Car," to promote how distinct it was going to be from the traditional GM organization and products. A team of ninety-nine union leaders, engineers, and managers studied world-class manufacturing and design by benchmarking organizations across the globe.

General Motors made Saturn a wholly owned company instead of a separate division of GM. It located the plant in Tennessee, where no other GM facilities were located, in order to give it independence. The UAW was recognized as the bargaining agent with the full support of the company before any cars were built, but instead of falling under the seven-hundred-page national agreement, the local union negotiated its own separate twenty-eight-page agreement which focused on firm governance and decision-making rather than on job descriptions.

After only two years of production, and for six years afterward, Saturn led domestic car lines in consumer ratings based on vehicle quality, reliability, and satisfaction after one year of ownership.[17] Saturn's rating each year also exceeded that of all other brands worldwide, with the exception of the much costlier luxury lines of Lexus and Infiniti (as well as Acura and Mercedes in 1997 only).

How did Saturn attain such remarkable results? And did the union-management Collaborative Partnership contribute to that level of quality performance?

Local union leaders were involved in a set of labor-management committees that met weekly to discuss the global auto industry, Saturn's corporate strategy, marketing, supplier selection, retailer relations, technology, product design, quality systems, and other "business decisions" that typically were the exclusive domain of management in the rest of GM. Equally important, the production system included no individual positions on the assembly line. Instead, all production workers were members of teams—engine team, transmission team, paint team, cockpit team, and so on—and these teams decided how their jobs or positions would be designed and organized in the manufacturing and assembly process and also how each team member would rotate around all the positions on the team. In addition, each team met weekly to discuss the team's quality performance, productivity, and safety, as well as how team members could improve their process and product. Finally, half the management positions in the company were filled by union members who were chosen for their skills and abilities in a joint selection process agreed to between the union and the company. Therefore, half the managers were represented by the UAW, and the other half were non-represented managers. They were also partnered to one another, so every represented manager had a non-represented partner, with the partners sharing an office and responsibilities. In the rest of GM, non-represented supervisors managed production, and union grievance committeemen handled "people problems"; but at Saturn, union-represented managers and non-represented managers were responsible for both.

To understand the Collaborative Partnership structures at Saturn it is helpful to differentiate between off-line and on-line processes. *Off-line* meetings (away from production) took place through weekly committee meetings between UAW leaders and Saturn management; the on-line work partnered represented and non-represented managers to run daily operations. In a parallel way, the Saturn workforce directly collaborated with one another off-line through weekly problem-solving and improvement meetings and on-line through self-directed work teams rotating between jobs or positions in the production process.[18]

Our research at Saturn showed how the local union added to firm performance through its role in creating and sustaining a Collaborative Partnership with management and by focusing its network of union leaders on production and quality as well as on member representation. Social network analysis at Saturn revealed a dense organizational communications network among the union leaders who held co-management positions. These union members communicated frequently within and across departmental lines as they worked on quality problems and other issues related to the production process.

A balanced allocation of time managing people and production—for both represented and non-represented managers—was a factor producing the highest levels of quality. In addition, departments in which union and nonunion partners had high levels of alignment on priorities, tasks, and responsibilities also resulted in higher quality levels than departments in which alignment was lower. But most important was the communications network infrastructure—particularly the communications between the union-represented managers. Our analysis showed that the communication and coordination network of the union-represented managers was much denser than that of the non-represented managers, and thus had a greater effect on quality performance. We found that the alignment between the union and management partners, the balance of time spent managing people and production, and the communications between union-represented managers were responsible for 30 percent of the variation in first-time quality and 53 percent of the variation in quality improvement.

This finding is strikingly similar to the results of our study of the spread of learning and innovation at the ABC School District in California covered in chapter 3; it was the union leader network in both cases that made an impact on organizational improvement. At Saturn the impact was on quality and at ABC it was on the sharing of innovation across the district. In neither case could we find a parallel in the non-represented management organization. The lesson is clear: unions in Collaborative Partnerships can add significant value to the performance of an organization through the network infrastructure they create—in ways that traditional managers cannot.[19]

The case of Saturn provides several lessons for other organizations and industries, including public education, that seek to create Collaborative Partnerships:

- The local union at Saturn took on responsibility for quality performance, and the union-represented managers saw quality management as part of their jobs. Thus, the union added value by taking on managerial responsibilities and bringing their expertise and independent perspective to problems, thus adding to the performance of the company by increasing the quality of decisions and the effectiveness of their implementation.
- At the same time, this process required a reinvention of the local union roles and responsibilities. To effectively represent the interests of its members, the union had to balance its mandate to negotiate and enforce the employment contract with its role in co-management.
- Further, Saturn developed innovative ways not only to build a partnership between union leaders and management but also to involve the entire workforce in extensive collaboration through both on-line and off-line teams on the shop floor.

Despite these innovations and successes, the politics of both the UAW at the national level and GM eventually undermined the stability of the partnership arrangement in Saturn. The management system and the union contract outlined earlier were so different from those in the rest of the corporation and national union that they were unsustainable as an "island of innovation." No organizational learning mechanism had been built to bring information and knowledge about this experiment back to either parent organization. Ultimately, the corporation and the national union opted for greater control (managerial prerogatives and contractual) rather than support the innovative work systems and employment relations that produced greater productivity and quality, albeit with less top-down control from the corporation or national union.

LESSONS LEARNED

This history is important because it has taught us important lessons that have informed collaborative improvement efforts in public schools, especially in the New Jersey Collaborative Partnerships to be described in part IV.

The Power of Collaboration

The first lesson is that something real is happening here: this is not a flash in the pan, an academic exercise, or the dream of a few idealists. The move toward greater employee engagement, extended partnerships, and flexible problem-solving has been growing for decades in a wide range of settings, including the leading companies of old manufacturing industries and new high-tech industries. Despite many obstacles and failures, the current continues to flow, because leaders in these organizations have become convinced that the wider engagement of employees and outside stakeholders is essential to success. In a world that demands increasing innovation and responsiveness, those organizations that can get everyone aligned in a general direction will inevitably do better than those that stick to the bureaucratic model in which everyone focuses just on one piece.

As applied to public schools, this suggests that education can be more successful if teachers, administrators, and school boards are all pulling in the same direction. When teachers are just carrying out mandates from above, they are not as successful—and the whole system operates less than optimally.

The Importance of Dense Communications Networks

A second lesson from these collaborative efforts is that the bureaucratic communication patterns—in which information flows up the hierarchy and commands flow down—are too restrictive to respond to the rapidly changing demands of a globalizing environment. Complex problem-solving processes often require the input, cooperation, and coordination of people across the organization. This calls for a dense network of communication, in which information can flow laterally and cross boundaries quickly as needed, and decisions can originate close to the point of implementation rather than making a laborious circuit up and down a hierarchical structure.

This shift requires changes in both formal structures and informal relationships. The extensive use of cross-functional teams and task forces forms the structural core of collaborative organizations; trust and shared purpose form the relational core.

As Mark Granovetter argues, economic activity is embedded in networks of social relationships.[20] Social network theory describes how such relationships impact behaviors, beliefs, and decision-making as employees make decisions and take actions not as individuals but within a social context.[21] The study of networks complements the study of individual attributes of employees when seeking to understand the dynamics of an organization—dynamics that play a key role in the performance of the organization. Coordination through informal networks enables information sharing across organizational boundaries. Tacit knowledge of employees in one unit is linked to employees in other units. As a result, units are able to work together to solve problems, improve quality, support innovation, and lower costs.[22]

The supervisory function in this type of organization is radically different from supervision in traditional Scientific Management–driven organizations. The function of supervision has evolved from controlling the work force to managing organizational boundaries.[23] Effective supervisors are valued less for their problem-solving ability than for their ability to support and provide resources to their teams. One of the key findings in our own research, therefore, has been the extent to which employees view collaborative supervisors as resources.

We saw in the evidence in chapters 2 and 3 that the deliberate development of communication networks across schools contributes to learning and innovation among teachers and that local union leaders in partnerships can play a key role in developing those networks. We also saw that teachers in those environments are more likely to see their leaders—both principals and union representatives—as resources. And as we described in chapter 2, public schools, like the companies we have just described, find that these systems of Collaborative Partnership lead to better organizational performance.

System Improvement and the Use of Task Forces

One of the key concepts of the quality improvement movement in both the United States and Japan is the distinction between system maintenance and system improvement. System *maintenance* involves making things flow more smoothly and efficiently along currently prescribed paths. System *improvement* means changing the paths—innovating, adapting, restructuring processes to respond to changing demands or to lift the organization to a new level of performance.[24] The most successful organizations, like Saturn, strive for both through *continuous* improvement: they don't settle for dealing with one problem at a time but constantly seek out opportunities to get better.

A central tool for quality improvement is the use of task forces. These go by different names such as *Quality Circles*, but they are all in essence groups of employees who work together but go off-line to do in-depth analyses of sources of problems and opportunities for improvement. Task forces can also bring together employees from multiple parts of the organization, in order to gather people with knowledge to contribute to the analysis.[25]

This is a fundamental violation of bureaucratic principles, which require that any communication across the organization pass through bosses up and down the hierarchy. For that reason, the use of task forces and cross-functional teams has been very hard to implement. People from different functions are not used to talking directly to one another, they are uncertain of the limits of their decision-making authority, and they don't know how their activity will be evaluated. They also have to learn new skills for managing discussions among people with different skills and reaching decisions through agreement rather than persuading a boss.

There has been a tremendous amount of learning. In successful collaborative organizations, most employees these days know how to develop an agenda, assess capabilities, do problem analyses, assign responsibilities—all things that in a bureaucratic system are done by the boss.[26]

In the New Jersey Collaborative, we have put strong emphasis on the use of "Improvement Initiatives"—another name for task forces—that take on projects to improve teaching and learning, bringing together multiple roles and functions. These have been very important in steadily raising the capabilities of these schools over time.

Shared Purpose

A striking shift in many large companies has been the spread of strategic discussions. Classically, strategy was kept tightly under wraps—a secret for the top leadership team alone, under the rationale that it was a source of competitive advantage. But the result was that most employees didn't know how their activities fit into the overall strategy; all they knew was their little piece.

With the spread of flexible teams and task forces, it became apparent that this wouldn't work: people had to have a picture of the shared purpose in order to coordinate their contributions to improvements. So it has become common practice to hold strategic discussions throughout organizations.[27] Some of these have become very elaborate, involving many employees over substantial periods of time.[28]

Schools have the great advantage of natural alignment—that is, pretty much everyone involved cares deeply about the education of children. But it is rare to have discussions of what is meant by this and what are the key strategies for improvement.

Thus a challenge for collaborative school systems has been to find time for the kind of strategic discussions that can yield major improvements in performance. There is no magic solution; it's a matter of steady learning. In later chapters, we will discuss some of the techniques that have been learned in districts across the country and in the New Jersey Collaborative.

Changing Union Roles

The cases of union-management partnership point us to the need to develop new roles for unions and their leaders. The most advanced partnerships, in which unions share the management function and accept responsibility for organizational performance as well as employee representation, go beyond the traditional arguments that unions add value through the balance of bargaining power, industrial jurisprudence, or disciplining of labor and management. Instead, these partnerships show that local unions have the potential to provide an infrastructure for the kind of communication and coordination network needed to produce the flexibility and responsiveness required of today's high-performance organizations. We explored this theme at length in chapter 3.

The Difficulty of Culture Change

It is evident from this history that moving beyond the limits of bureaucracy is very hard. Many companies we have dealt with have been working on it for decades. They have tried radical tactics, such as cutting entire layers of management to force decision-making downward; but more often, it has been a matter of slow, unsteady experimentation.

Many managers put the issue in terms of the need for "changing culture." The problem is that no one quite agrees what culture is, still less how to change it. It involves at least two dimensions: a set of values shared across the system and a set of routines, or habits, that implement those values. Shifting those shared expectations often arouses resistance, because people like the way things are done now; or it may simply cause confusion, because there is no longer agreement on how things should be done. Top-down efforts to redefine these complex patterns of beliefs and routines are always too rigid and simple to work; people have to work many things out for themselves in their own contexts and sets of relations.[29]

One lesson we draw from these experiences is that change requires patience. But we have gone a bit further than that. Rather than focusing on defining the culture or "mission," we find it is better to initiate groups working on changes they perceive as important and then to encourage reflection on that process.

The elaboration of peer discussions is a major piece of culture change. By increasing deliberate lateral discussions through learning networks— what we call a "web of support"—we find that we can accelerate the development of agreement on how to do things. These webs are able to work through the details of emerging cultures—how people should act in particular conditions—with far more flexibility and granularity than any kind of top-down training curriculum. It is still a slow process, but also more adaptive and resilient.

The Need for Broader Scaffolding and Support Systems

The Saturn case in particular reinforced a larger lesson: isolated cases of partnership rarely spread, and they suffer from constant pressure from the broader system operating on different principles. It is therefore key that these innovative models have a "web of support" rather than existing as "islands of innovation." Bridges must be built between sibling organizations, and exchanges must be encouraged between them. Support must come from parent unions and management executives.

Here public school systems start with an advantage. The local leaders at Saturn had no way to get their story through the vast hierarchy above them to the General Motors Board of Directors. In the case of our public education system, however, democratically elected local school boards offer a much more realistic opportunity to showcase the benefit of Collaborative Partnerships for student and educator outcomes.

CONCLUSION

Collaboration and partnership remained separate through most of the twentieth century. The dominant philosophy of Scientific Management, and the bureaucratic model of organization, explicitly rejected worker involvement.

At the same time, the American view of labor relations was an adversarial game of limited partnerships. Neither party wanted to feel indebted to or dependent on the other. Occasional exceptions at both levels were promising and sometimes dramatic, but they remained isolated.

Over the past fifty years, the value of bureaucratic management has been deeply questioned throughout society; workers have increasingly sought meaning beyond the paycheck, and managers have increasingly seen the value that can be brought by engaged workers. Unions, initially resistant to collaborative efforts, began to revisit the question of labor's involvement in managerial decision-making. And the network structure of local unions is preadapted to offer more flexibility and responsiveness to hierarchical organizations. As a result, there are more instances in which partnership and collaboration have come together in a new organizational pattern. In the next chapters, we will explore the development of Collaborative Partnerships in school systems.

CHAPTER 5

Collaborative Partnerships in US Public Education

T HE HISTORY OF COLLABORATION in public schools is shorter than in industry. Among other things, the neoliberal policy track of the past forty years has generally disempowered teachers and school leaders. Nevertheless, there have been important efforts in a scattering of school districts across the country, running against the tide in a collaborative direction.

Despite the adverse policy environment, the educational sector does have some advantages in moving toward collaboration. First, as mentioned earlier, there is a natural consensus on the basic goal, which is not the case in most companies. Pretty much everyone cares about the development of children, while not everyone cares deeply about the quality of steel.

Teacher unions also start with some advantages over the private-sector examples we have reviewed:

- Both national unions—the National Education Association (NEA) and the American Federation of Teachers (AFT)—support efforts to involve their local association leaders and teachers in joint governance and greater collaboration with administration and school boards.

- Educators are not typically subject to the cyclical changes in labor markets, wages, and employment security that are features of the industrial world.
- Finally, the education sector is largely governed by locally elected school boards. If union-management partnerships and educator collaboration lead to higher-quality education and student achievement, then parents can elect board members who want to build these arrangements into their school districts.

Collaborative Partnerships during the neoliberal period since the 1980s have necessarily been special isolated cases: they work outside the general norms and policy framework. They inevitably resulted from unusual circumstances, such as crises, or leaders with strong beliefs. A few, such as the ABC Unified School District case (mentioned earlier but described in more detail below), have survived for long periods; others have withered when leaders have changed or the initiating impetus has faded.

Most of these past partnership efforts have been centered on one particular partnership: between school administrators and teacher unions. These are the two "frontline" players in the education system. Thus it is not unusual for local superintendents and union leaders to develop relatively cooperative personal relationships, which can sometimes blossom into more systemic collaboration over time. For this reason, our stories here will be primarily about union-management partnerships, though the New Jersey Collaborative has been focusing on developing a broader multi-stakeholder system (see chapter 9).

The potential for collaboration between teacher unions and administration directed at school improvement is an area that has gone largely unexplored in the literature of school reform. Some researchers have suggested that a quality partnership between district management and the local union may help to create an environment conducive to teamwork and professional community, based on the assumption that reform will be more sustainable when labor and management share the same vision and agree on the appropriate course for carrying it out.[1] Our own studies, reported in chapter 2, are among the only ones to go beyond single cases to show evidence across multiple districts of the positive effects of union-management partnerships on both students and educators.

But there is value, as we mentioned, in looking at case study material that can go deeper than these quantitative studies. Julia Koppich has studied three "reform bargaining" school districts in which collective bargaining contracts extend well beyond wages and working conditions into education policy and the quality of teaching and learning.[2] We add here examples drawn from six school districts we have studied around the country, to illustrate how innovative districts can foster collaborative approaches to curriculum development, scheduling, budgeting, strategic planning, hiring, subject articulation, interdisciplinary integration, mentoring, Professional Development, and evaluation, among others.

We show how these efforts were created and sustained and what they can teach us about the impact of significant involvement of faculty, staff, and their local union leadership, working closely with district administration, to share in meaningful decision-making and restructure school systems.

Six Districts: A Summary

The six school districts featured in this chapter were not chosen at random for our research and are not intended to be a representative sample of all school districts nationally. Rather, they were chosen for study because of their lengthy track record of innovation and because they appeared to have institutionalized, long-term Collaborative Partnerships between administration and the local teacher union.

All six districts had sustained Collaborative Partnerships for at least ten years at the time of our study. In other ways, however, they were highly diverse. Some were urban, some rural; some wealthy, some poor. They were located in different sections of the country, from California to Florida.

Although all had union representation—some by NEA, others by AFT—some were in right-to-work states and lacked bargaining rights.

We visited all of these districts and interviewed union presidents, school board members, superintendents, central office administrators, principals, union leaders, teachers, support staff, and members of the community. In addition, we studied their collective bargaining contracts, memorandums of understanding, student performance data, and relevant internal reports.

We have reported on these studies in more detail in earlier publications.[3] Here, after a brief description of the cases, we focus on the lessons we learned from them in terms of what worked, and what needed to be worked on, to develop the New Jersey Collaborative described in part IV.[4]

ABC Unified School District and the ABC Federation of Teachers (California)

The ABC Unified School District, located about twenty-five miles south of Los Angeles, was featured in chapters 2 and 3. Its twenty thousand students were linguistically and ethnically diverse, and approximately one-quarter of the students were English language learners. At the time of our study over 45 percent of students qualified for free or reduced-price lunch. The district employed 927 teachers throughout thirty schools, including fourteen Title 1 schools. The history of collaboration in the ABC District goes back to the 1990s and has continued, and indeed grown, through several changes of superintendents and union leaders.

After fifteen years of Collaborative Partnership, student performance (then based on California's Academic Performance Index, or API) was well above the state average, with 90 percent of the students graduating, and 85 percent going on to college.

We reported in chapters 2 and 3 on our in-depth studies of the ABC District, which included surveys, observations, and interviews over several years. At the time of our case studies, we saw ABC as among the most advanced partnership districts within our exceptional cohort, but it also provided variation in the levels of school collaboration.

Florida

The district we studied in Florida was one of the largest in the United States, with over twenty-five thousand employees and two hundred thousand students. The student population was economically and ethnically diverse. Fifty-eight percent of district students qualified for free or reduced-price lunch. The district had experienced a strong and mutually supportive partnership among district administrators, the board of education, and the teachers union for more than forty years, dating back to the late 1960s.

This district had among the highest graduation rates in the state, especially among large districts, had achieved an "A" rating from the state based on student achievement three of the previous four years, and had doubled its Advanced Placement enrollment numbers in that period.

Virginia

In Virginia, we studied a district with thirty-six thousand students and more than three thousand teachers. The partnership had developed over thirty years.

During our study period the district continuously improved its performance in all subgroups on tests of Adequate Yearly Progress, and more than half the schools met all benchmarks. The district had an overall high school graduation rate of 80.4 percent. Sixty-four percent of the students received free or reduced-price lunch.

New York

Our study in New York was in a largely rural district, with close to two thousand students and three hundred teachers and other professional staff. More than 50 percent of the students received free or reduced-price lunch. The partnership began in the mid-1970s.

During the period studied, student performance was above state averages in language arts, math, and science, and the high school graduation rate improved from 72 percent to 88 percent—well above the state average. Eighty-five percent of graduates continued their education beyond high school.

Minnesota

This school district had approximately 5,500 students and 350 teachers. Twenty-eight percent of the students qualified for free or reduced-price lunch. Theirs was one of the newer partnerships in our sample, dating to the mid-1990s.

In the year of our study, the district proficiency scores in reading and math were above the state and county averages and above all neighboring districts but one. Students in grades five through nine had improved their scores by about one year against national comparisons over the previous four years; the district was named one of the twenty most improved by the Minnesota Department of Education. The high school graduation rate was 96 percent, and college attendance grew from 60 percent to 76 percent over the previous six years.

Ohio

This was a large urban district, employing two thousand teachers and educating twenty-five thousand students. Approximately 75 percent of district students received free or reduced-price lunch. The district's partnership dated to the early 1980s.

Compared with the other large urban school districts in the state, this district had the highest graduation rate and was a top performer on state performance measures. One of the district's specialty schools ranked in the top 10 percent of US high schools according to *US News & World Report*. In 2001, the district and the local union earned a major award for innovation from the John F. Kennedy School of Government at Harvard University.

THEMES ACROSS THE COLLABORATIVE DISTRICTS

Despite the diversity of the districts in terms of size, wealth, and geography, there were a number of striking similarities. First, all of them had exceptional levels of performance. We didn't select them initially for that reason—we were just collecting partnerships of long standing—but all stood out in their cohorts on standard measures of achievement, including state tests results and graduation rates. Though the selection was not random, this fact adds to our confidence that Collaborative Partnerships generally support strong performance.

Second, partnerships in all six districts focused explicitly on the improvement of teaching and learning. These partnerships often had their origins in conflicts over compensation, resources, or other contentious issues; but the parties worked through those conflicts by turning to their shared commitment to the students, and they built steadily on that base. The battles that continued to dominate most of the education system—teacher pay, curriculum, mandates, processes—became secondary, and solutions could be worked out as the stakeholders became increasingly convinced that they were all pursuing the same basic goal. In each of these cases, a culture was built with improvement of teaching and learning at its core.

While we began our research with a focus on union-management partnership, we became more aware that the systems in these districts combined this institutional partnership with deeper educator collaboration. In all cases, the processes began with union and management leadership but penetrated over time deep into the ordinary work of teachers, administrators, staff, and often parents and school boards. Large percentages of teachers were involved in district- or school-level committees or teams, or as mentors, teacher-leaders, master teachers, or Professional Development trainers within the collaborative process. In the New York case, union leaders estimated that *every teacher in the district* had participated in at least one team, committee, or department/grade-level leadership role.

We also became increasingly aware of the importance of communication among teachers, within and across schools, in developing new ideas and spreading new practices. We explored this theme in detail in our research in the ABC District: as we saw in chapter 3, the network of teaching-focused collaboration among teachers was twice as dense in the stronger partnership schools compared to the weaker partnership ones, and this difference was directly linked to the adoption of classroom innovations. While we did not conduct such rigorous studies in our other districts, we were astonished by the richness of collaborative interactions. In Florida, hundreds of (union-appointed) teachers served on committees discussing Professional Development, curriculum, and dozens of other issues; and hundreds more served as peer trainers or teacher-leaders at a grade or department level. In Virginia, a dense network of teachers dedicated to school improvement was created through faculty participation in peer assessments and discussions of teacher quality, student-data teams, school-based leadership teams, and initiatives to improve teaching quality and capacity. In Ohio, hundreds of internal teacher-consultants to the Peer Assistance and Review evaluation process have (as one said) "changed the conversations" by focusing on teaching quality.

To an outsider, the degree of collaboration was remarkable; educators visiting these districts were particularly impressed that they were able to find the *time* for all the apparent "add-on" meetings and responsibilities. But we came to understand that in these cases, the collaborative mechanisms were *not* "add-ons"; as one union president explained, they were just "the way we do business in this district," the regular process for getting things done. One cannot understand the operation of these districts without grasping that they are indeed different *systems*, with different expectations and habits.

The systems performed well because they produced far less friction than normal. By *friction* we mean the typical misunderstandings, suspicions, cross-purposes, and resistances that inevitably characterize bureaucratic systems. People in these collaborative schools were more aligned on the basic purposes and were constantly developing together the core strategies and processes for improvement. When decisions were made at the top levels, people all through the system were normally aware of the intent and the reasons and were supportive in implementation.

This had not always been the case, of course. The initial transition to a collaborative approach was typically rocky and full of friction. The parties, with long histories of mistrust, needed to go through a process of testing out one another's commitment, making sure that they were not walking into a trap, and seeing the meaningful results of the new way of working. There were, as various people told us in similar language, many "bumps in the road." Because we chose to study districts with a collaborative history of at least a decade, we were seeing them after they had smoothed out many of those bumps and after the system had consolidated into shared values and common practices.

The themes developed in the research—the shared focus on teaching and learning, the depth and breadth of participation, the growing density of communication networks—have taught us a great deal. We also discovered a more specific set of mechanisms that helped create and maintain these Collaborative Partnerships.

We have built on all of these lessons and experiences in developing the collaborative model in New Jersey that we outline in chapter 8. We sketch these lessons below in categories that we developed gradually over the course of the research and our later practice. We begin with operational systems—the ongoing work of the districts. Then we will turn to what we call "scaffolding"—the support systems that maintain the collaborative culture, especially institutions that extend beyond a single district.

Operational Systems

The typical operation of collaboration, as we analyzed it, started with institutional *partnership*: the early phases were almost entirely built around meetings and relationships between union leaders and top administrators. These operated in parallel to the regular operations of union committees and management hierarchies. Over time, they evolved into a more complex system that included far more than that limited partnership group.

As the systems matured, a governance system developed on two foundations: *stakeholder-based support committees* and *improvement initiatives*. The stakeholder-based support committees were standing groups at the school and district levels, meeting regularly to manage ongoing processes such as planning and leading the system overall. Improvement initiatives were more bounded and temporary groups focused on particular innovations, ranging from new curriculum to peer assessment of teaching; they aimed at developing *improvements* to the system rather than ongoing operations. Some, such as the Peer Assistance and Review Process in Ohio, later became an ongoing part of the new district system. These initiatives were composed of people at all functions and levels who could make important contributions to that task. This distinction between support and improvement mirrors one we saw in chapter 4, drawn from the quality improvement literature across many industries, between system maintenance and system improvement.

No two districts used exactly the same structures or the same terminologies, but they all ended up in roughly the same place: with stable committees at the levels of districts and schools, bringing together a variety of key stakeholders in regular discussions of ongoing systems issues and a set of improvement initiatives focused on raising the bar.

Partnership

The origin and central pillar in all these districts was always the union-management institutional partnership. In every case, the early phases of the collaborative effort were marked by increasingly close relations between the leaders of the administration and the union. In the ABC District, for example, the superintendent and union president began a tradition of meeting for lunch at the same time every week, with no set agenda—just to keep one another informed and to share any issues before they grew into serious problems. In Florida, similarly, weekly meetings between the leaders expanded to regular union-management meetings at all levels. Perhaps more important, all the districts reported a great increase in informal contacts—quick calls, dropping by the office. This changing norm greatly reduced friction and made it easier to anticipate changes or to brainstorm new initiatives.

Unions began to provide extraordinary support for the collaboratives. In Florida, the local union appointed hundreds of members to committees and leadership roles. In Minnesota, the local union vice president developed a plan for a Teacher Academy focused on teacher quality and Professional Development, which would be run collaboratively by the union, administration, and school board. Starting in Ohio and then spreading to other states, the union coordinated Peer Assistance and Review programs in which teachers visited one another's classrooms and provided feedback and mentoring. In New York and in the ABC District, the national union provided training, and administrators and union attended sessions together.

Over time, these partnerships drew in other key stakeholders. In Ohio, for instance, representatives from the administrators' union also joined the conversations. School boards were brought into formal committee roles in three of our cases. In four cases, parent representatives became part of standing committees and major strategic discussions. The union and administration in several cases worked actively to promote school board candidates who appreciated and supported the collaborative process. In these and other ways the support systems for the collaboratives began to extend beyond the walls of the districts, bringing in independent stakeholder groups whose voice and engagement was important for the ultimate quality of education.

These partnerships always remained as the supportive skeleton of the collaborative effort but over time developed into deeper collaborative structures and processes.

Governance and Oversight Teams

Eventually, these districts established a broader model of shared governance, in which formal joint planning and decision-making forums allowed the union and administration, and other stakeholders, to work together and align the strategic priorities of the district. They also developed an infrastructure that gave the union leaders and members significant input in planning and decision-making on issues such as curriculum, Professional Development, textbook selection, school calendar, pedagogy, and schedules. The act of managing was viewed as a set of tasks that leaders (both union and administration) must engage in for the benefit of teachers and students.

All the districts in their own ways developed new permanent mechanisms for the coordination and maintenance of the collaborative system—typically at both school and district levels and involving multiple stakeholders. The ABC District had regular meetings of key district and union partners, which we describe more fully later in this chapter; they also had regular joint meetings of the union executive committee and the superintendent's cabinet. Florida had School Site Steering Committees that discussed issues such as the budget, best practice instruction, class size, dress code, applicant screening, and teaching assignments. Virginia, in addition to district and school teams, had teams at every grade level focused on student evaluation. Their school-level teams regularly developed comprehensive accountability plans jointly among the teachers, administration, and parents. In the New York case, the District-Wide Educational Improvement Council included teachers, administrators, union officials, and parents to facilitate shared decision-making, joint planning, goal setting, and implementation.

Improvement Initiatives

Each district also had teams focused on particular improvement projects. These were generally overseen by the various governance groups, and sometimes those groups themselves took on major projects; but in many effective instances, the improvement projects were spun off into independent, focused teams, with a different set of members appropriate to the problem.

It is difficult even to summarize these efforts, as they multiply and morph rapidly from year to year. In the ABC District, an early collaborative improvement project focused on a set of high-poverty schools with low reading test scores. Committees from the schools worked with district and union leaders and parents to improve hiring practices, strengthen curriculum and instructional methods, build support at home, and expand Professional Development. Later committees took on textbook adoption; interviewing prospective administrators and teachers; a new program for peer assistance, mentoring, support, and evaluation; new teacher orientation; and processes for data-based decision-making regarding student performance. In Virginia, schools had School Improvement Process (SIP) Teams that focused on student performance and took up best practice instruction and teaching assignments, among other issues.

Other examples of collaborative improvement projects included in our sample give just a taste of their range and scope:

- teacher academies focused on Professional Development
- curriculum integration across grade levels
- methods for sharing instructional practice
- greater teacher input into Professional Development
- school safety initiatives
- developing and implementing new block schedules
- introduction of computer-based teaching technology
- sophisticated systems for analyzing student achievement data to better focus student interventions

We should again emphasize that these were *improvement* projects—not just maintenance. When the collaborators discussed, say, school safety, they were not just trying to make incremental changes or tighten efficiency; they were analyzing the root causes of the concerns and looking for solutions that would lead to significant qualitative improvement.

Many of our study districts took on major initiatives to improve teaching through peer feedback and sometimes peer assessment. In Ohio, the union president was at the forefront in proposing an innovative teacher-led Peer Assessment and Review system that supported new teachers through a rigorous mentoring and evaluation process and also helped veteran teachers improve their practice. Extensive Professional Development was offered by teachers who served as internal consultants. In Minnesota, the Collaborative developed a performance improvement system that established customized Professional Development led by teachers through twelve year-long courses in the Teacher Academy, or through cross-disciplinary, teacher-led study groups that were encouraged to innovate, take risks, and actively improve their practice.

A particularly striking improvement project was the development in one district of a "Walkthrough Protocol"—a shared process to assess schools, teachers, Professional Development, and each school's Comprehensive Accountability Plan. This process involved teams of administrators and teachers visiting other schools to evaluate student performance and pedagogy and then giving feedback to stimulate a professional dialogue. The Walkthrough Protocol was designed to be a model based on nonthreatening peer-to-peer review and collaboration. It promoted the idea of the district as a learning community within and across schools: administrators and teachers worked together to identify strengths, weaknesses, and best practices in each school and develop joint solutions for improvement. Extensive participation by faculty in the student-data teams, school-based leadership teams, and initiatives to improve teaching quality and capacity created a dense network of teachers across the district dedicated to school improvement.

Ongoing Participation

As these governance and initiative systems developed, the districts developed a rich array of discussions on the whole range of topics central to the improvement of education, involving large percentages of the teachers and administrators along with representatives of other stakeholders.

Again, we take just a few examples. Four years after the introduction of the Student Performance Improvement Program in the Minnesota case, 90 percent of teachers in the district had elected to participate. They established networks that continued to bring up new ideas and to spread them widely through the system. In Ohio, as mentioned earlier, the web of internal consultants, or facilitators, for the Peer Assistance and Review process continued to develop new proposals for curricular articulation and integration. The idea of a "facilitator network" became instrumental in the efforts to grow this work in New Jersey, as described in part IV of this book.

In general, these districts—all of whom, it will be recalled, had been developing collaborative systems for at least a decade—had passed a tipping point in which broad participation was generally expected. And because collaboration had become a habit, major conflict was rare. People had developed levels of trust, skills, and knowledge to work through their differences in ways that advanced their common focus on the improvement of teaching and learning.

Scaffolding

Scaffolding is our term for mechanisms that support the collaborative system, from both inside and outside the districts. These can include leadership teams above the district level, skills training and other workshops that bring in outside knowledge, regular meetings among collaborative districts, Professional Development, and outside consultants or internal facilitators.

On the whole, these were much less developed in our study districts than the internal operational systems, particularly in the early phases. Our study cases were all basically one-district operations. Many of them made catch-as-catch-can use of existing workshops—in several cases run by national unions—that taught meeting management, shared decision-making, problem-solving, and other important skills. The ABC District and the district in the New York case made use of internal consultants and trainers from the American Federation of Teachers.

In several cases, the collective bargaining process was used to scaffold the collaborative system. New York and Minnesota included union involvement in key committees in their contractual agreements. The local contract in the Florida case was based on an assumption of collaboration in decision-making and had called for union appointments to all district decision-making committees since the early 1970s, starting with textbook selection and Professional Development. The contract set a baseline, though the parties had moved beyond it: the union became involved in decision-making even if the issue was not explicitly stated in the contract, because the board policy and the district culture was one of inclusion and shared governance.

Virginia presented another interesting case: it is a Right-to-Work state with no formal bargaining rights, yet the parties established a set of written memoranda of understanding on collaborative procedures that provided a stable framework for the effort.

Over time, most of these districts also recognized the importance of engaging the community. They involved community members or parent groups in school-based governance structures or in district-level planning processes, as described earlier, and they supported school board candidates who were favorable to collaboration. This paid off in a number of key battles in which the community and school board supported the teachers in pushing back against budget cuts or onerous mandates.

As the districts matured, they became less dependent on particular leaders and built some of their own scaffolding—in particular a deep bench of internal leaders developed through experience with the collaborative process and often good relations with school boards. In the case of the ABC District, this became evident in their New Principal's Academy, which provided Professional Development to administrators. And as we have seen, collaboration in these districts became increasingly a system intertwined with every aspect of daily operations and culture. Thus when the original leaders did leave, there was internal broad support for the continuation of the Collaborative.

Some of the districts received support externally from the Teacher Union Reform Network (TURN), which provided opportunities for districts to exchange experiences, and others got support from the American Federation of Teachers, which gave technical assistance and helped spread the Ohio system of Peer Assistance and Review among other districts.

On the whole, however, these districts were isolates: none had much interaction with other Collaborative Partnerships. In our terms, they lacked the scaffolding of a strong ongoing network of peers. They were thus vulnerable, especially in their early years or when their key leaders changed.

Two Problems

These districts were, by definition, outliers: we chose them for our research precisely because they stood out as islands in a sea of bureaucratic systems.

Thus, in at least two respects they do not serve as good models for a wide-spread scaling of a collaborative system: (1) they required extraordinary crises to achieve initial takeoff, and (2) they depended heavily on exceptional district leaders.

The Problem of Leadership

Probably the most important scaffolding element, notable in every one of these cases, was unusually stable and committed leadership. In three of our cases, the key union leader had served in that role for more than thirty years (which might allay the political concerns of union leaders considering Collaborative Partnerships!). Superintendents were also generally quite stable across this cohort.

But this fact presents a problem in developing a *generalizable* model of Collaborative Partnership: not all districts can count on that kind of stability. These districts relied on leaders because their innovations were *unusual*: we picked them specifically because they stood out as islands of innovation.

Under such circumstances, the outside institutions—government departments of education and regulators, national unions, state-level associations—were often uninformed about the collaborative efforts, and sometimes hostile. Teachers and administrators were wary at first of letting down their defenses: they wanted proof that it would be worth it. So the role of strong leaders was crucial: they needed both to stand up against outside pressures and persuade their internal constituents that change was for the best. But strong, convincing leadership was a solution needed for pioneer cases, not for a broader extension of the model.

For these reasons, we have *not* drawn the obvious conclusion that strong, charismatic leaders are essential to Collaborative Partnerships—even though they were essential to these six cases. Instead, in order to generalize the model, we have drawn the lesson that more scaffolding systems are needed that are capable of supporting less extraordinary leaders—who may not have exceptional capabilities.

Thus we paid a great deal of attention in the New Jersey Collaborative to developing scaffolding mechanisms, as we will see in chapter 8. These started with a multi-stakeholder support group of state-level leaders from the key education associations—School Boards, Superintendents, Principals and Supervisors—as well as the state-level union organizations. These associations played a key role in encouraging and supporting their members in the early, difficult phases of collaborative development. We also developed a curriculum that included the standard skills of meeting management and consensus decision-making but also treated issues more specific to Collaborative Partnerships, such as the design of governance committees and problem-solving for initiative teams. We focused on governance structures at both the district and school levels to support and institutionalize this work. And finally, we had learned the value of a network of peer facilitators to anchor this scaffolding.

We have found, in the ten-year history of the New Jersey Collaborative, that these mechanisms can sustain the system through the changing dynamics of leadership succession and the inevitable tensions of the start-up phase. We will discuss some of these instances later—for example, when the hesitancy of a new superintendent is surrounded, one might say, by their Superintendents' Association, their teachers and their union representatives, their own principals and their association, and perhaps even their school board. At that point it would take an extraordinary leader to *resist* the path to collaboration.

The Problem of Initial Motivation

There was one other common characteristic across our study sample that we do *not* want to build into a model: all of them originated in major conflict and crisis. Five of them experienced a strike or a vote to strike at or near the start of their Collaboratives; in the sixth, the union president sued her superintendent at the culmination of a bitter battle. These crises were important in convincing the parties that there must be a better way, bringing them to a search for common ground.

But to develop a collaborative alternative to the neoliberal model, we do not want to incite conflict across the entire education system. Fortunately, that doesn't seem to be necessary. We now have hard, peer-reviewed, and published evidence that collaborative systems benefit students and educators. There is also now enough dissatisfaction with the policies of recent decades that many people are looking for something better. In New Jersey, the state-level association leaders had the personal networks to encourage some of their members to join even without a major crisis, and as the New Jersey Collaborative has grown, the success of its members has drawn in new districts in a positive snowball effect. So we are confident that the growth of the approach can sustain itself organically.

CONCLUSION: A MORE PRODUCTIVE PATH TO REFORM

The six school districts in this chapter demonstrate that unions, administrators, and school boards can choose Collaborative Partnership as a means to find new ways to improve the performance of the district, teachers, and students. The partnerships are clearly vehicles for system improvement, not ends in themselves. We believe this is a more productive path for reform than the market or bureaucratic strategies that have received so much attention from policy makers in the past. This chapter describes contexts that produce the conditions for Collaborative Partnerships to take root, the strategies they employ to impact teaching quality and student performance, the structures that promote broad participation, and the factors that have allowed them to endure over decades.

We have scattered throughout this chapter some of the key lessons we have drawn from these cases. To summarize:

- We learned that collaboration is not a program but a gradually developing *system*, with many parts. It generally starts with a good relationship between two leaders forming a partnership, but if it lasts, it extends deep into the organization and changes the way many things are done on a day-to-day basis.

- We learned the importance of building dense webs of interactions across teachers and other stakeholders, to share learning and new ideas for improving the system.
- We learned that there need to be mechanisms both for maintaining the system—daily problem-solving and management—and for improving it through focused experimentation and innovation.
- We learned that, as islands of innovation, these systems were fragile and might not withstand the loss of the charismatic leaders who created them.

Therefore, for Collaborative Partnerships to be sustained over the long term and to have a meaningful impact, they must be institutionalized—built into the systems of the district in both policy and practice and protected from those who benefit from perpetuating the myth that administration and unions, by nature, want different outcomes for students. These systems must also be surrounded by a "web of support" that builds capacity and supports these innovative new strategies, structures, practices, and culture.

In reflecting on the national cases in this chapter, we wondered whether stability could also be established by moving beyond the dependence on individual strong and inspirational leaders through the establishment of *networks* across districts, so that they are not isolated and can understand and learn from the experiences of their peers and generate interest in this work from their parent organizations. We also wanted to explore how we could build capacity through a network of local leaders who could serve as peer facilitators across multiple districts. We will describe how this has been attempted across districts and schools in New Jersey in part IV.

CHAPTER 6

The Changing Union Role

THIS CHAPTER IS ADDRESSED primarily to one particular stake-holder: unions, in their role as partners. We focus on this issue here because it is too rarely discussed. Entry into partnership often requires significant change in roles and structures for unions and their leaders. It can be controversial. It involves moving away from the simple pursuit of one set of members' interests to a more complicated strategy of advancing those interests by strengthening the system as a whole. It can become a political flashpoint: sometimes challengers emerge with a call for more aggressive attacks on management.[1]

At the same time, we have seen in the previous chapters that union involvement in partnerships has often succeeded in meeting member needs while also improving the system. Increasingly, union leaders in traditional businesses have recognized that participation in what has been considered managerial work creates opportunities for greater influence in decisions that run the business. Since the late 1970s, an increasing number of unions have been willing to accept those opportunities to participate in managerial decisions, understanding that in doing so, they are giving the members they represent a seat at the table.[2]

We researched such efforts in detail in a study based on interviews and observations in twenty local unions with deep involvement in worker participation efforts, drawn from the auto, steel, airline, pharmaceutical, glass, health-care, defense, papermaking, and garment industries as well as higher education and municipal government.[3] We have continued with further studies of 261 local union leaders in nine public school districts. The research reported in chapters 3 and 5 of our large nationwide sample of school districts, and our work and research in an ongoing effort involving twenty-five districts in New Jersey, have added further data.

We have found in these varied studies and cases that involvement in Collaborative Partnerships requires significant changes in the structures and strategies of local unions and in the skills and roles of their leaders. Members need to be persuaded that a collaborative approach leads to a better workplace. Local representatives need to learn how to engage in problem-solving and decision-making discussions with management. The local union typically needs more internal committees and mechanisms for dialogue. The transformation of workplaces is not contingent solely on management changing its mindset; in unionized industries, the unions must be prepared to transform themselves.

There is also a risk of tensions with the national or state union, which may not understand the strategic value of partnership engagement or may find it threatening to the work done over decades in building a strong but traditional collective bargaining agreement. We described this in chapter 4 when we discussed the experience of the United Auto Workers local and the Saturn Corporation with the national UAW and General Motors. In that case, the desire for control by both the parent company and the national union undermined the innovation and success achieved by both union leaders and managers at the local level. This tendency for control and centralization is an ongoing concern in the long run for any Collaborative Partnership.

But the upside is increasingly important. In an era when private and public sector unions are experiencing severe threats, successful partnerships bring critical advantages. They can result in increased involvement of members, especially younger members, and improved relations with the community. And most of all, they can improve the work lives of teachers and staff, by elevating their voice, reducing the level of mistrust and top-down control, and enabling a focus on what teachers care about most: the improvement of education for their students.

COLLABORATION INCREASES MEMBERS' SUPPORT FOR THEIR UNIONS

We start by pulling together findings from our research that, together with the experience of the union leaders in the New Jersey Collaborative, suggest that collaboration strengthens unions.

First, in Collaborative Partnerships, unions are directly involved in constant discussions with administrators about how to make work better, which results in visible improvements in teachers' daily experience. As a local leader in New Jersey put it, "We do have a seat at the table and we're no longer looking into the window or mail slot." And we reported earlier the finding that collaboration increases members' job satisfaction. When members feel better about their jobs and see their representatives actively involved in the improvements, they are likely to see their union as more relevant and constructive. Our research shows that union members in strong Collaborative Partnerships are much more likely to see their union leaders as a resource, people to turn to for advice and support.[4] Collaborative Partnerships also lead to an increase in members' human and social capital—their own skills, knowledge, and professional relationships—which again strengthens this sense of the union as a positive agent in improving working life.[5]

Further, we saw in chapter 3 that union leaders in Collaborative Partnerships develop much richer networks of relationships with their members, both within and across schools: they become central nodes of exchange about teaching and work life. This is the kind of relationship that most unions can only long for; their connections to members are typically limited to those with grievances, rather than the majority who want to develop a positive workplace.

Thus it is not surprising that local union leaders in the New Jersey Collaborative effort have found enormous benefit from their engagement in the partnership. As one such leader said,

> Over the past seven years, our building has experienced a culture shift. The best part was that we found that our younger and newer staff decided to volunteer or run for union positions. They became keenly interested in this idea of union-management collaboration because they're a generation that grew up believing that their voice mattered and they wanted to add their voice to the conversation. And the other nice benefit was that our veteran staff decided to re-enter their voice into the conversation. So they came, too.

THE UNION LEADER'S ROLE

The union-management partnerships described in the earlier chapters have resulted in a new set of roles for union leaders with regard to their functions and responsibilities. School district union leaders engaged in these partnership arrangements have found that their responsibilities extend beyond the traditional roles of contract bargaining and enforcement through the grievance procedure to active leadership in school improvement. This shift of responsibilities mirrors the earlier expansion of union leader roles in industrial firms as documented in our research. We see this expansion of roles in both our qualitative and quantitative data.

Over the past ten years, we have surveyed 261 school-level union leaders in nine districts about their leadership roles.[6] In school districts with weak or nonexistent partnerships, school union leaders reported their primary roles to be communicating about bargaining issues and enforcing the contract through the grievance procedure—the traditional roles of school union leaders. However, in districts with strong union-management partnerships, school union leaders reported that they have added important new roles to their traditional responsibilities for bargaining and grievance handling. These new responsibilities include

- ensuring teachers/members have a voice in decision-making about school policies and educational quality,
- ensuring that teachers/members in their building have forums to participate in school-level improvement, and
- communicating with teachers/members about school improvement across the district.

This transformation of union leader roles is illustrated in figure 6.1.

Union leaders in collaborative settings, in other words, focus on more than collective bargaining and grievances; they need to keep more balls in the air. They balance their more traditional responsibilities for contract negotiation and enforcement with new responsibilities for ensuring teacher voice in decision-making and problem-solving concerning educational

FIGURE 6.1 Partnerships change union leader roles

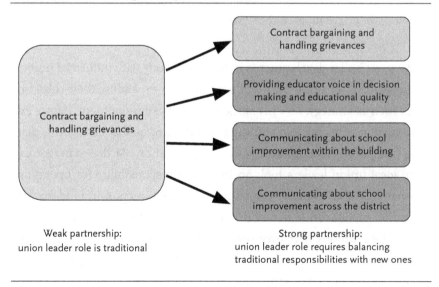

Contract bargaining and handling grievances

Contract bargaining and handling grievances

Providing educator voice in decision making and educational quality

Communicating about school improvement within the building

Communicating about school improvement across the district

Weak partnership: union leader role is traditional

Strong partnership: union leader role requires balancing traditional responsibilities with new ones quality and school improvement. Broader participation by union members and their leaders in problem-solving and decision-making leads to (1) higher-quality solutions and decisions as a result of the participation of those with deep knowledge of the issue; (2) more problems being solved, as more people are involved in the improvement process; and (3) greater support for implementing solutions with fidelity, since people will support a decision in which they have ownership. Therefore, by creating and maintaining Collaborative Partnerships in an organization, unions in these new roles are adding tremendous value.

A local union leader in NJ described her experience:

> Before I was union VP I did Grievances and I was busy a lot. It's important to note that in our building we have not had even a level 1 Grievance in five years. In the district we have a Grievance Chair who previously had been so overworked. Now, every time we have our monthly Executive Committee Meeting, he says, "Nothing to report." So, he's helping with other things. That isn't to say we'll never have one. But we went from lots of grievances to they don't exist. Because we take care of the problem before they have to reach that level.

We saw similar developments in our 2001 study with industrial unions. At the governance level, most of them reported expanding their roles into areas such as strategy, new investments, product development, choice and introduction of technology, training, job design, quality assurance, planning, supplier selection, and work reorganization. At the management level, local union leaders took on increased responsibility for operations "co-management," supervising and directing production in tandem with nonunion supervisors and middle managers. Many leaders as well as others in their local unions were involved on a regular day-to-day basis in making operating decisions that used to be the sole domain of management.

Our 2001 study revealed an emerging view by local unions of managerial "prerogatives." Local leaders were rethinking the concept of management, separating managerial work from the people who do it. Management itself increasingly was seen by a majority of the leaders in the study as a function or set of tasks, not as a separate class of employees; in these local unions, leaders and members were getting more deeply involved in the tasks of governing the organization, strategic decision-making, and running the operation on a daily basis.

These new responsibilities have required new capacities for local unions and their leaders. They need to take an active role in problem-solving efforts with management. A superintendent said: "What's really important to me is that the union president and his team always come with possible solutions. And then we sit together as a team and go through the solutions." For union representatives to gain this kind of credibility and influence, they need to develop deep skills in problem identification, data analysis, and joint decision-making. And in order to implement those solutions, they need knowledge of planning, project management, and other tools.

But they also back up those capabilities with new ways to mobilize and organize their members to share their voices through the partnership. We saw in chapter 3 that union leaders in collaborative districts become network builders: they engage in more interschool communications and sharing of innovations between schools. They also are more deeply involved with the members they represent in communicating about ways to improve their schools.[7] This density of union leader communication networks benefits the internal solidarity of the union as well as contributing to the continuous improvement of classroom practices. We see this in the finding that in stronger partnerships, members are more likely to see their union as a resource to them.[8]

A local vice president in our 2001 study put it this way:

It took a while, and I think it's an ego thing more than anything else, for me to be able to go to an area of the shop and say, "I have a problem in your area, I need my union members to figure out how to cut 40 percent of the scrap you're generating in there, because it's one of the goals that the company needs."[9]

A school union leader in New Jersey said:

We've all been trained how to fight. We have not been trained how to collaborate. And that's the difference here.

A state-level union leader explained the shift in more detail:

In places like this, collective bargaining states, where for literally 40 to 50 years, we and every one of our statewide partners have spent a good part of that time teaching our constituencies how to win through advocacy and to fight. And we're really good at it. And it doesn't matter whether you're the union or you're a school board or you're the principals or the superintendents: we have all spent a lot of time fighting about things that we all cared about, and we were just using the wrong processes to get to those things we all cared about.

So I would offer that here in New Jersey, the things that we're doing as part of this work around labor-management collaboration are about learning, re-learning, unlearning the things that many of us have been taught through our years of experience.

Yet the union leaders we studied also emphasized strongly that it is not a matter of simply moving from an adversarial approach to a cooperative one; it is a matter of doing both. The introduction of shared problem-solving involves a careful balance. A school union leader put it:

It's been a willingness of the people involved to kind of set the adversarial part aside. Not throw it away: they still have their roles. They still file a grievance when a grievance needs to be filed, they still have arbitration, they still bargain—but they do it in a different way. . . . We still absolutely protect our members. But it's not the gotcha anymore.

Leading an Empowered Membership

Union members who participate in leadership teams and improvement initiatives gain a new sense of confidence. This sometimes means that they feel empowered to push back not only against management but also sometimes against their own union leaders. A story from a recent Diversity, Equity, and Inclusion initiative illustrates this dynamic, in which the sense of psychological safety developed in a collaborative system enabled members to voice uncomfortable feelings that often remain buried:

> This year, we decided to focus solely on equity. We approached our equity initiatives this year thoughtfully and earnestly. But something unusual happened to us. About midway through our year, several of our team members who are of color took a risk: they expressed strong concerns that maybe some of our efforts could actually have the opposite effect of what we had intended, that without expertise to navigate the difficult conversations, more hurt could come to the people who had already been hurt, and it could be another false start.

This could be a treacherous moment for union leaders: if they responded defensively or insisted on exercising their authority, they could undermine trust with their own members and create internal fissures. But in this case the union, with its partners, gained by taking a collaborative stance:

> So we paused, we sought professional guidance, and we revised our plans. Now, that honesty that came from the members would never have happened in a traditional model.
>
> Collaboration for us over the years has established psychological safety so that those members could share their vulnerability. And with that came authenticity and then true progress, which will lead to sustained change instead of being caught in that model of a top-down initiative that results in just checking a box and moving on.

INTERNAL STRUCTURES AND MECHANISMS OF INVOLVEMENT

The need to balance these multiple roles has led to structural changes in the unions. The typical structure of an executive board and a representative council—with occasional meetings at each level—has proved to be too thin to manage the rich array of teams, improvement initiatives, and governance meetings that develop in collaborative systems. The elected union representatives can't do it all. Rank-and-file teachers and staff have become directly involved in many of these meetings and tasks. As local unions take on increased responsibilities for firm management and governance, they also face increased accountability for their roles in managerial decision-making. Members working on task teams become accountable for tasks that were formerly the responsibility of administrators.

As the union has become involved in more levels and types of decision-making, it has needed to provide representatives to connect and partner directly with managers, such as the director of curriculum or the business administrator or the superintendent. For example, here is a list of the extensive regular standing meetings developed over many years between union and management representatives in the ABC Unified School District, described in earlier chapters:

Administration		Union
Superintendent	↔	Union President
Chief Financial Officer	↔	Chief Negotiator
Assistant Superintendent Human Resources	↔	Union President / Chief Negotiator
Assistant Superintendent Academic Services	↔	Peer Assistance & Support System Coordinator
Curriculum and Professional Development	↔	Liaisons for Elementary / Secondary

Administration		Union
Director of Secondary Schools	↔	Vice President Secondary
Director of Elementary Schools	↔	Vice President Elementary
Director of Special Education	↔	VP Special Education / Special Ed Advisory Committee
Coordinator of Child Development	↔	VP Child Development
Information Technology	↔	IT Liaison / Union President
District Administrative Cabinet	↔	ABC Federation of Teachers (ABCFT) Executive Board
ABCUSD Principals	↔	ABCFT Site Representatives

Source: "Building Partnerships to Create Great Public Schools," California Labor Management Initiative, CDE Foundation, June 2022. https://cdefoundation.org/staging/wp-content/uploads/2017/01/CALMI-Jun22-Resource-Guidebk-DIGITAL-FINAL.pdf.

Many roles on the right-hand side of this list are new to most union locals as are the relationships with the administrators on the left-hand side. And that is not even the whole of it: there are also large numbers of committees, both regular and temporary, in which unions and their members gain a voice.

All this activity requires bringing more members into leadership roles and structuring internal discussions and training for those leaders and other members who participate in the collaborative processes.

In chapter 3, we described the way union leaders in the ABC Federation of Teachers (ABCFT) created a dense network that helped share learning innovations across the school district, especially in schools that had developed strong partnerships between the union and administration. We argued that this network brought enormous educational value to the district and was built on the institutional structure of the union as an organization.

The ABCFT supported its leaders through capacity building and internal organizing to strengthen both the local union and also its role in the partnership with administration. They did this by promoting between-school relationships through monthly union meetings that brought union representatives from different schools together into dialogue on a variety of issues, including school-level problems and relations with school leadership. School union representatives reflected on district-level initiatives and the implications for their schools. These meetings served as natural platforms of knowledge and information sharing. The agenda always included both the representational needs of members and the role of the ABCFT in the partnership.

The local union also partnered with the administration to sponsor learning events and innovation projects designed to promote teacher collaboration, student learning, and community engagement. In annual districtwide conferences organized by the union and management partners, presenters had opportunities to share school-level innovations that educators had recently undertaken. One year, a school presented its newly developed "Mathucation" program, which creatively interwove physical education and mathematics standards. Other schools presented diverse initiatives jointly conceived and implemented by teachers and administrators, ranging from effective classroom technology to parental outreach and involvement in afterschool activities. The evolution of these school innovations became a common topic of communication in the conferences, both formally in group discussions and in private.

These events, conducted as part of meetings open to the public, provided an effective platform for sharing and encouraging learning between the district's schools. They provided a conduit for dissemination of school-level innovations. Critically, however, they also provided a platform for direct relationships to form and strengthen between schools. For example, during meals and breaks, union representatives and principals from different sites could sit side by side and communicate. As the formal, overarching theme at many events was sharing progress concerning both the partnership and school-level improvements, many informal communications were pursued "offstage." And some events included group exercises that assigned union representatives and principals to teams with counterparts from other schools.

BARGAINING

A common concern of union leaders in collaborative efforts is how to relate these activities to collective bargaining. The cooperative problem-solving at the core of collaboration seems like the opposite of the solidaristic militancy needed for effective bargaining.

That hasn't been the general experience, however. It's always hard to say what might have resulted from strategies that weren't pursued, but union leaders engaged in collaborative efforts have not had noticeably more trouble getting good contracts than their more traditional counterparts.

The natural counterpart to operational collaboration is "Mutual Gains" or "Interest-Based" bargaining. Traditional bargaining assumes mistrust and seeks to gain a unilateral edge through bluffing and manipulation. Mutual-gains bargaining instead seeks to turn the process into a shared problem-solving effort based on trust between respected adversaries. This is, of course, philosophically more in line with the principles of collaboration. But does it work in terms of advancing the interests of union members?

The vast literature on bargaining strategies doesn't help much in answering the question. We are unable to find any studies that directly compare the effectiveness of mutual-gains and traditional negotiation—that is, there are plenty of single-case stories on one side or the other, but no studies that compare across a large enough sample to yield good general conclusions.

We saw earlier, however, that collaboration yields many benefits for union members and for the union as an institution—including more trusting relationships, richer communication links, lower voluntary turnover, greater commitment and engagement in the profession, improved job satisfaction, and social capital, not to mention positive effects on achievement for the students. That's a lot of what bargaining would hope to accomplish.

In effect, the ongoing discussions in the many collaborative forums effectively take on some of the tasks that have normally been done in occasional bargaining: working out creative solutions or developing shared improvements in work life. A local union executive board member in New Jersey explained:

> We recognized early on that there needs to be a balance between advocating for your lens and inquiry. That's allowed us to work together to ask questions, to understand what the pressure points are on each of the roles in the district that deliver for our students and our student families. And it's helped us to be really effective in being able to frame our communication to our members in the association, to the community.

In another district, a union leader reported:

> The Instructional Council changed from just being reports by the administrators to the teachers, to the administration bringing up decisions they are talking about making so we can have a say in the decision-making process, not after it's already been made.
>
> We're starting now where we're going to have the central administration staff meeting every other week with a union member to discuss things so we get more say and an idea of what's taking place, sharing out our successes to the whole district as to what we're achieving.

These are the issues that typically get crammed into the last few minutes of collective bargaining sessions, up against deadline pressure, and become bargaining chips rather than efforts to find optimal solutions. By instead dealing with them in frequent extended discussions, these schools achieve better outcomes for all the parties.

But this still leaves some of the core collective bargaining issues: wages, benefits, and job security. The normal operation of partnership doesn't touch these, which is the reason periodic bargaining is still important. All we can say is that we have seen no evidence, in our own research or experience or that of others, that Collaborative Partnerships yield worse outcomes on those dimensions than other types of systems. On the contrary, there are occasions when partnerships definitely do better: in several of the cases we described in chapter 5, administrations supported teachers in their concerns about wages and security, which may have made a difference in the views of school boards.

As one New Jersey principal put it,

> I think we respect the Collective Bargaining Agreement more. And I think we're more proactively working toward avoiding any conflict for sure. I think our conversation between administration and association is a lot less about job conditions. It's about teaching and learning. That's what our conversation is about most of the time. And so, it's a pleasure. You know, we don't always agree. But there's a real clear common goal when you're talking about focusing your attention on student success.

Some bargainers try to use partnership as a bargaining chip: they threaten to withdraw from the partnership in order to force concessions from management. But the experience has been that the damage done to the partnership relationship is more harmful for union members than any gain that might result at the bargaining table. Two leaders from our 2001 study told instructive stories. One was from a local leader with the American Nurses Association:

> We did hold back from the labor-management committees ahead of negotiations without a reason, but to show that leverage, that we're going into negotiations more and quit cooperating. And that lost our credibility with the management as well as with our own members. So I think what we realized to go forward is that if the teams are working and if you don't have a reason [to] quit cooperating, go forward, don't use that artificial leverage of showing them what it would be like without you. You got to have a reason. [S]o if communication or collective bargaining modes break down, then it's the time to go back to those teams that think they got a good thing going, and show them the bigger picture, and then ask them to stop their cooperation. But you can't do it just for leverage.

And one was from a local union coordinator from the Steelworkers:

> We were threatened with a strike, and our leaders in the partnership
> process became our strike captains, used their networking skills, so it
> really turned things around for us. . . . [On the other hand] . . . we pulled
> our support for a partnership just a few days before the contract was due
> to expire. In hindsight I think it was a mistake. I think you can do more
> when you are in the room than when we were out of the room."[10]

POLITICAL RISKS

Many union leaders, when considering partnership relations, are concerned
about the political dangers of involvement. This is a realistic concern. We
have observed a number of cases over the years, in multiple unions and
industries, in which local presidents spent so much time and energy building relations with management that they lost touch with their members—
and it cost them elections to more militant challengers.

Such failures are relatively rare, however. As mentioned earlier, three of
the six union leaders in the cases described in chapter 5 had been in office for
thirty years or more at the time of our studies. In the twenty-five New Jersey
districts participating, we are aware of only one election in which support
for the Collaborative Partnership effort was a major campaign issue—and
in that election, the supporters of partnership won overwhelmingly. In far
more cases, support for the union and its leadership grows as the members
see it involved in issues that concern them daily on the job, and as they see
its value in supporting their participation in improving the system.

We have often noticed that the most dangerous approach politically for
a union leader is to take a reluctant, hands-off, ambivalent position toward
partnership. That pleases no one: it diminishes the effectiveness of Collaborative Partnership without solidifying internal solidarity. The benefits
are most evident when the union is most involved in visibly making a
difference with management on problems important to the membership,

improving education for students, strengthening its internal networks, and engaging more of its members in collaborative committees. Union leaders are likely to gain influence from those advances, which accounts for the many cases of long tenure for those who take an active role in Collaborative Partnerships.

CONCLUSION

For all these reasons the collaborative effort has received strong support from union leaders at the national and state levels. At a 2021 conference on Collaborative Partnership in New Jersey, NEA President Becky Pringle said:

> NEA is committed to leading a movement to unite our members and this nation to transform public education into a racially and socially just and equitable system that prepares every student to succeed in a diverse and interdependent work environment. Building a nationwide system that fosters and supports labor-management collaboration is essential to that vision.[11]

And NJEA President Sean Spiller added:

> When we invest in this work, we know we are engaging in work that will continue after we are gone or when there are changes in the district. . . . The work continues because we know the value of it. It's built on respect. It's built on relationships. It's built on work that is constantly ongoing to make sure that this is successful for our students.[12]

We leave the last words to a local union vice president in New Jersey:

> Committing to this collaboration model empowers all of the stakeholders. It's not a zero-sum game. It renders our union more relevant. It becomes like a twenty-first century model of what a union can be. It gives us as a

union, as well as the administrators, the superintendents, and the boards of education, increased power, but not because of fear, instead because of mutual respect.

The future of our union can and should be in our own hands. Collaboration, like any kind of authentic partnership, is messy. It's not a straight path. But it's worth the effort, because professionals shape the direction of their profession. And we all want to be professional.

PART IV

The New Jersey Collaborative: Developing a Model for Reform

WE TURN NOW TO the building of a network of Collaborative Partnerships in New Jersey. Earlier in this book we have drawn on the lessons from past experiences, emphasizing some of the most important aspects of successful efforts. But these have been isolated and exceptional experiments, dependent on unusual leaders and relationships. We have developed some aspects of design, structure, and scaffolding that, we believe, can create a *generalizable* model of Collaborative Partnership, scalable to entire states, and potentially replacing the neoliberal approach that has dominated the last four decades.

We start with a brief overview of the New Jersey effort over the past ten years, which includes twenty-five districts as of this writing, with plans to add further districts in coming months. Then, in chapter 8, we elaborate details of the model, including the techniques for starting new efforts, the core operational elements, the support systems that help sustain these efforts, and considerations for spreading to large scale. In chapter 9, we discuss the lived experience of the districts—their difficulties and obstacles, learnings and new developments, and leading-edge challenges at this time.

CHAPTER 7

The Case of the New Jersey Collaborative

A single courageous State may, if its citizens choose, serve as a laboratory; and try novel social and economic experiments without risk to the rest of the country.

—Louis Brandeis, Associate Justice of the Supreme Court, 1932

IN MAY 2013, a group of leaders of the key New Jersey state education associations met at the Center for Collaboration in Work and Society at Rutgers University. They included representatives from the New Jersey School Boards Association; the New Jersey Principals and Supervisors Association; the New Jersey Association of School Administrators (superintendents); and the two teacher unions, the New Jersey Education Association and the American Federation of Teachers New Jersey. We presented to them an early take on the research sketched in chapters 2–3, drawing lessons from existing experiences of Collaborative Partnerships in public schools and showing the link between collaborative relations and student achievement.

At the time there was no clear plan or proposal to start such an effort in New Jersey. But the association leaders, impressed by the research on impact and by our cases of success across the country, committed to trying union-management partnerships as a way of creating more collaborative systems and processes in New Jersey school districts. With Rutgers they formed an informal State Support Group to identify promising districts for pilots and to encourage their members to take part.

This turned out to be a fortuitous way to start, although we didn't fully appreciate it at the time. There was little support from the state government: the governor was pushing a strategy of privatizing public education, expanding charter schools and vouchers, and relying on top-down mandates and high-stakes testing, as described in chapter 1. But we have since learned that similar efforts that started with foundation funding and heavy dependence on government support often have difficulty sustaining a strong connection over time to the people leading education at the state level and institutionalizing practice in districts and schools. Such efforts have tended to prioritize large, well-funded conferences and training sessions but have had less emphasis on building networks with state associations to engage local districts and schools in the deep work of trust building and systems change. The New Jersey State Support Group, by contrast, had little funding but a great deal of influence and deep relationships with many districts, and the group was critical to recruiting the first cohort of schools.

The New Jersey Public School Labor-Management Collaborative (as the effort was later named) held several Capacity Building Workshops with six districts in its first year. The focus was on helping district leaders to plan, design, and implement two basic collaboration structures—a District Leadership Team and several School Leadership Teams—and to initiate problem-solving around some initial projects to improve teaching and learning in their district. The effort took off quickly. For example, within a year in one central New Jersey district, the School Leadership Teams in the high school and a middle school had built strong trust, had completed some initial projects that showed the effectiveness of collaborative relations, and were engaged in defining new and more ambitious projects.

Nineteen additional districts went through the Capacity Building Workshop over the next seven years. They developed their own Leadership Teams and began improvement projects—but each in its own way. Some were driven primarily by the district leaders, some more from the school level; some took on ambitious projects, others moved more cautiously; some hit obstacles and conflicts and needed further support. The operation continued on a shoestring, with a Facilitation Team, which consisted of the authors and several colleagues from the university, leading the initial workshops and providing some ongoing facilitation; but it rapidly became clear that this team could not carry the growing load.

This pressure led to two further innovations. In 2016, the Collaborative sponsored the first Interdistrict Learning Network Conference. The primary purpose was to give all the districts involved an opportunity to reflect on their work and exchange information and experiences with other districts. It began with an introduction by the state leaders and the Rutgers Center, followed by presentations by the first districts in the Collaborative on the role and functioning of the District and School Leadership Teams, along with open discussion from the floor. The district-level leaders from all the districts then met in one breakout session, and the school-level leaders in another to exchange their experiences, problems, and obstacles, as well as their successes and innovations. Later, in another breakout session, the members of each district discussed what they had learned and developed plans for next steps.

Interspersed with these discussions were some presentations on leading-edge tools and concepts that had not been discussed in the first round of Capacity Building Workshops or that were being surfaced as issues arose in multiple districts. These included "leading from the middle"—a way that organizational innovation can spread from experiments at multiple levels of the organization—and "Interest-Based Bargaining," presented as a complement to collaboration for contract negotiations. In the breakout sessions, these concepts mixed with the experiences and concerns of the participants to help generate new ideas and initiatives.

Another element of these interdistrict meetings consisted of "role-alike" discussions, in which people with similar roles in different districts—union leaders, superintendents, principals, board members, teachers, and so on—met together to share their experiences. This process often produced more candid conversations and brought out issues that were not voiced in meetings with the other parties. We found that collaboration needs such private venues to bring out issues that may otherwise be hidden.

The Interdistrict Learning Network rapidly became a major piece of the "scaffolding" contributing to the strengthening of the effort. We encountered many instances in which districts found new energy in these meetings and went home to launch innovative initiatives or resolve ongoing conflicts. The Interdistrict Learning Network Conferences, which have been held twice a year since 2016, shifted to an annual virtual format in 2021 and 2022 during the pandemic when they set new participation records, with well over three hundred people attending each conference.

The second major innovation was the development of a Facilitation Team from among the educator participants in the initial collaborative cohort. This was in contrast to the method used in many efforts, both in industry and education, that rely entirely on specialized outside consultants. The difficulty of this approach was documented in a 2000 report on collaborative "whole-school reform," which found indications of success but identified as a weakness the continuing high cost of consultants, as well as the use of rigid, complex standardized curricula that were difficult to adapt to local circumstances.[1]

The New Jersey Collaborative took another tack, bringing together sixteen leaders from some of the early adopting districts for a facilitator training workshop in summer 2017. These included teachers, union leaders, principals, superintendents, supervisors, and school board members. The topics included systems change, drivers and resistance, the facilitator role, governance structures, mission statements, project management, problem-solving, decision-making, conflict resolution, and other central issues and skills. The workshop introduced concepts from many traditions, such as Quality Improvement and systems dynamics. The Consortium for Education Change introduced its decision-making framework, based on the work of Patrick Dolan.[2]

From that point on, this Facilitation Team has been central to the development of the Collaborative. In subsequent Interdistrict Learning Network Conferences, members of the group made presentations on the experiences of their districts, including progress, obstacles, and innovations, which generated new ideas among the participants. The Facilitation Team led discussions on topics such as "What kinds of projects/initiatives have been most effective for School Leadership Teams (SLTs) and District Leadership Teams (DLTs)?" and "How do schools and districts assess and measure their progress?" The Facilitation Team has also taken a lead role in every district and school Capacity Building Workshop from 2017 to the present. Through their participation in these workshops, the facilitators have also become known to new district leaders as valuable resources and mentors and have developed strong relationships with these peers. The facilitators sometimes receive phone calls for guidance and advice and have hosted or visited new districts to provide support. We have held Facilitator Training Workshops every June since 2017, and the Facilitation Team has grown in number.

The *interdistrict learning network conferences* and the *peer facilitators* developed into a "web of support" that helped sustain districts through the inevitable challenges of transitioning from a top-down bureaucracy to one of rich internal collaboration. This forms, we believe, the essential scaffolding that has enabled the New Jersey Collaborative to overcome the isolation of the collaborative efforts described in chapter 5 and the fragility of many similar efforts around the country that did not long survive. As of this writing, ten years after its launch, the New Jersey network has grown steadily, with virtually no dropouts.

In 2016, the Collaborative began prioritizing bringing in large urban districts with higher poverty levels. These presented some new challenges, but we found that the basic mechanisms—the Leadership Teams, the Improvement Initiatives, and the Web of Support through the Facilitation Team and the Interdistrict Learning Network—worked effectively in these settings.

The COVID-19 pandemic slowed new capacity building in school districts for two years, although the Facilitation Team was able to conduct some virtual training sessions. However, the efforts in districts that were already in place continued at full speed. We were delighted to learn that many of the districts had used and developed collaborative mechanisms to navigate the COVID crisis. We will describe some of these cases in more detail in chapter 9.

Meanwhile, the success of the Collaborative began to attract outside attention. A delegation of national leaders of education in South Africa visited six times over six years to study the work of the Collaborative as a potential model for their country. Representatives from other states began asking to attend the Interdistrict Learning Network Conferences and other events. Governor Murphy offered his support in an address at Rutgers in 2018.

In September 2021, the US Secretary of Education, Miguel Cardona, came to visit one of the districts in the Collaborative: the Delran Township School District. He watched while leaders and facilitators from several districts of the Collaborative spoke of their experiences and what they had learned. Cardona expressed his support, especially stressing the evidence of student performance improvements gathered by the leaders in Delran, as well as from our other studies:

> Being in education for twenty something years I've seen examples of good collaboration, I've seen examples of poor collaboration, and at the end of the day I've never seen it connected to student outcome results the way I saw it today. . . .
>
> You're intentional with developing systems that will outlast you in your roles. I believe strongly, and I've seen it here: focus on the process and the product will follow. You develop good processes built on trust, collaboration, respect, some of those basic things that we expect, right? And you embed that in your systems and the product will follow. What product? Student outcomes most importantly. But as I said earlier, teacher efficacy, a sense of belonging, a sense of shared purpose . . . [3]

When the participants in the early cohorts reflected back on their journeys, they emphasized that the development of collaboration was anything but a straight line. We will describe some of the variant trajectories in chapter 9. There were periods when the process seemed to have plateaued, only to take off again with new energy. There were obstacles created by changing stakeholders: in one district, the superintendent was ambivalent for a long time, and the effort was driven by several principals and union leaders until a new and more supportive superintendent was hired. In another district, the leadership at the district level took the lead, but the effort came to a plateau after two years—until they realized that they needed to try some new approaches and initiatives to engage the school-level leadership. School boards were obstacles in several cases, though crucial supporters in others. Other districts thought they had become models of collaboration until some stakeholders pointed out gaps and challenged the leadership to deepen the effort. In all these instances, the enthusiasm and commitment of some key stakeholders as well as the evolving culture and structures kept the process moving while others gradually came to see its value—showing the importance of engaging multiple stakeholders and multiple levels for long-term progress.

CHAPTER 8

An Interactive Model for
Collaborative Systems Change

THE JOURNEY DESCRIBED in chapter 7 was not linear: there were many challenges and adjustments. Yet for all its messiness, the shift to Collaborative Partnership is a *deliberate* process of change, based on consistent principles and guideposts.

For as long as theorists have written about organization change, they have wrestled with the question, Should it be driven from the top of the organization, or should it be open and participatory? The top-down approach—starting with a solution and cascading it down through the organization—is the more comforting, especially for the leaders themselves, because it seems to promise control, predictability, and efficiency. The fact that many such efforts break down due to resistance, or run into obstacles unforeseen by the leaders, rarely leads to a change in thinking; instead, leaders often assume that they just need to find a better solution and try again. That has been the pattern of bureaucratic companies for well over a century. Management gurus such as Alfred Sloan and Frederick Taylor emphasized that only the managers could understand the whole picture and that those under them should never deviate from their instructions. As Taylor said, "Under our system, a worker is told just what he is to do and how he is to do it. Any 'improvement' he makes upon the orders given to him is fatal to his success."[1]

But those who have studied and worked in these efforts have generally concluded that organization change is more complicated and that wider engagement is beneficial. One major review of change strategies called for going "back to the drawing board"—reflecting the fact that employees at many levels and in many functions are needed for implementation of any solution.[2] Also, employees *know* things that top leaders don't. There are infinite numbers of stories about ideas that sounded great when preached from the top levels but elicited scorn and laughter from other levels that recognized obvious problems. These issues are detailed in a seminal *Harvard Business Review* article from 1990 with the challenging title "Why Change Programs Don't Produce Change."[3]

The potential benefits of wider participation increase as work becomes less routine, requiring more knowledge. Schools are of course archetypes of knowledge-based work: the frontline "workers"—teachers—have advanced degrees and must have sophisticated understanding of not only a substantive field but also methods of pedagogy. In such conditions, mandates from the top will at best omit valuable knowledge and at worst (and commonly) will undermine elements essential to success.

Some theorists have gone to the opposite extreme from the directive approach, formulating "bottom-up" concepts of change. But that approach doesn't really work either: those on the front lines cannot know all the issues that leadership deals with every day. So most who have studied this issue, especially practitioners who have actual experience of organization change, come up with some mix of top-down, bottom-up, and middle-out—a complex combination that is far less predictable than the directive approach.[4] Action learning, Sociotechnical Systems Design, Quality Improvement, and many other movements have explored such mixes since at least the 1960s. We have drawn on these traditions for our approach in New Jersey.

Our review of experiences of collaboration in education from across the country, summarized in chapter 5, showed us that all of these efforts—even those that had many successes—had trouble spreading beyond single districts. Often the reason was that they relied on one or two key supports—typically, an idealistic, charismatic leader. Some of the key innovations in the New Jersey effort are aimed in part at overcoming this barrier by creating a system of mutually reinforcing parts that can help sustain collaboration through changes in leadership and through inevitable periods of strain and conflict. These innovations include a multi-stakeholder support team at the state level, a web of peer support across districts and roles, and a focus on action toward a shared purpose of improving teaching and learning.

THE INTERACTIVE APPROACH TO CHANGE

We have called our approach to change *interactive* to emphasize the continual engagement of all stakeholders in open discussions and mutual learning. Others have used terms such as *participatory*. *Interactive* is admittedly a vague term by itself. As developed in the New Jersey Collaborative, however, interactivity in change efforts takes the form of a set of mechanisms and tools used systematically to build relationships and trust, key competencies, and structures for discussion and decision-making.

Basic Principles

The interactive approach involves many important values, including collaboration and trust. We focus here, however, on six interrelated, more specific principles that have been central to our approach:

1. A Focus on Improving Teaching and Learning

We view this as a purpose-driven intervention: everything is aimed at improving teaching and learning. The Collaborative is not primarily about improving the quality of working life, trust, or relationships—though those are certainly important to success. The focus is always on the outcomes for students.

Purpose has become something of a buzzword in management circles.[5] But schools have one great advantage over businesses: virtually everyone is deeply aligned on the basic purpose—everyone really cares about children and their development. Thus the Capacity Building Workshops from the very start emphasize that purpose and can largely take it for granted. It's just a matter of keeping it constantly in view.

2. Multi-stakeholder Engagement

A key starting point in many efforts has been a partnership between union and management.[6] In the New Jersey Collaborative, we have expanded this concept by building partnerships with *multiple* institutional stakeholders: unions, school boards, superintendents, and principals. They are represented on a support group of our state associations, and they form peer networks that help make sure the different perspectives are represented.

These institutional leaders have played several important roles: helping to recruit new districts for the Collaborative; persuading their members that the idea was worth trying; helping their members through periods of difficulty and doubt; and shifting the culture of their organizations, and the training provided to their members, toward a broader and more collaborative lens.

3. Webs of Peer Support

A distinctive aspect of the interactive model is that it is built very largely on peer interactions and support. It stands in sharp contrast to models that are driven from the top, usually by management engaging troops of consultants. Our approach is extremely light on traditional consultants, focusing more on developing facilitators from those who are actively engaged in the collaborative process: teachers, superintendents, union representatives, and school board members. The approach also brings districts together on a regular basis to share their experiences and concerns in regular learning meetings, with strong leadership from the peer facilitators. Finally, it develops role-alike networks, in which people can talk to leaders from other districts in similar positions about their problems and solutions: superintendents with other superintendents, union leaders with other union leaders, and so on.

This network of peers has at least two major benefits. First, it is very *resilient*. Traditional top-down models regularly fail when leaders change;

in contrast, webs of peer support, like the World Wide Web of the internet, can tolerate failure in one part because others can pick up the effort and find new paths of development. When new superintendents come in who are skeptical of collaboration, their peers in other districts, as well as the state-level superintendents' association, can work with them to build their trust in the process; meanwhile, individual schools within their districts that have become committed to the approach can carry it forward in their own ways. When school boards change course in political storms, super-intendents and union partners can work together to steady the ship. We have repeatedly seen districts that have encountered obstacles that would have doomed traditional efforts but have found ways around them through new combinations of actors. Thus there has been an extraordinarily high retention rate among the districts of the Collaborative.

Second, peer support networks are an *inexpensive* method of intervention. Outside consultants are extremely costly, and the costs tend to continue much longer than anyone expects. It is very common for internal actors to get in the habit of consulting with the outsiders: it is easy to shift blame if something goes wrong. Peers, by contrast, are naturally enthusiastic about helping their counterparts and building supportive relations. The peer networks are mutually beneficial: people learn from their peers as they are discussing their own experience.

Outside consultants, in the interactive model, play a catalytic role—primarily bringing new combinations of people together, secondarily help-ing to gather and articulate lessons that can be widely shared across the networks. In the New Jersey case, the total involvement of the Rutgers Collaborative School Leadership Initiative, which played the role of neutral convenor, has been approximately one day a week for a process that now engages twenty-five districts.

4. Prioritizing Action

Many collaborative change models start with culture, often by develop-ing mission statements. We start instead with an emphasis on *doing things—together.* The task is to make improvements in teaching and learning; structures, processes, and culture support that task.

A priority of the very first workshop for new districts is to begin defining potential improvement initiatives—projects that would significantly advance the educational mission. These early initiatives may be relatively simple, such as particular scheduling changes, experiments with interdepartmental teaching teams, or methods of sharing instructional practice. But even at the start, some schools opt to take on more ambitious topics like curriculum, performance, student behavior, or parental engagement.

We do not ask districts to develop mission statements at the start, because the guiding purpose—improving teaching and learning—is generally understood and uncontroversial. Later, once some collaborative projects are underway, differences may appear in what that means, and at that point it may make sense to stop and develop a written mission.

In general, our view is that culture follows action. People very seldom change their views by reading, studying, or even developing value statements. Many organizations of all types have value or mission statements that are widely ignored, even if they are taught in pedagogically sound training sessions and posted on walls everywhere. Culture is developed primarily through real interactions and efforts to achieve collaborative goals.

Prioritizing action does not mean *ignoring* values and culture. Culture frames everyone's expectations. It is important that people reflect on the ways things are done and the values that underlie these ways. The problem comes when culture and values are disconnected from practice and become merely slogans. Our approach therefore starts with trying to achieve collaborative goals and *then* proceeds to reflecting on values.

5. Attention to System Improvement

We focus primarily on the *system.* Individuals may experience personal revelations—a dramatic transformation of style toward more collaboration—but individual transformation has not been an explicit focus of the Collaborative. Rather, we have emphasized primarily a systems view: building new structures and processes to enable people, technology, buildings, policies, schedules, and the myriad other aspects of the educational system to work together for the benefit of the students.

We also draw attention to the *improvement* of systems. We have incorporated the Quality Improvement literature's distinction between system control and system improvement.[7] System control focuses on problems that are essentially imperfections in the current system; correcting them would strengthen the existing way of doing things and make things run more smoothly. System improvement is about transformation, doing things in a fundamentally different way for major advances in performance. The move toward collaboration is itself a system transformation, and, as the research shows, is associated with major performance improvements when done well. The mechanisms of the Collaborative—the workshops, processes, leadership teams, networks, peer facilitation, and reflections—encourage taking on difficult shifts that can make a dramatic difference.

6. Continuous Reflection and Learning

There is a fair amount of content to be learned in developing collaborative reform efforts: the structures of leadership teams; the management of improvement initiatives; shared frameworks for problem-solving, decision-making, conflict resolution, and other skills; and standard tools for commissioning and reviewing improvement initiatives. But this content is always adapted to the particular context and the practical needs. Each district, as we have already seen, develops its own version of the structures and its own approach to initiatives. After the first wave of enthusiasm, some find that they have reached impasses or plateaus or are unsure what to do next. These moments are opportunities for deepening understanding and moving to new stages.

Thus, the interactive approach builds in many opportunities for reflection on practice and experience: these include initial and ongoing Capacity Building Workshops, regular interdistrict meetings, role-alike sessions for people with similar roles in varied districts, and coaching by peer facilitators.

Workshops always include periods for assessing progress. These varied settings encourage districts to stop and review how things have gone and also introduce new ideas that might help move the Collaborative Partnership forward.

Key Elements of the Interactive Approach in New Jersey

The Collaborative has developed an array of structures and processes to implement these principles (table 8.1).

1. Initial Motivation

In our review of past cases of school collaboration in chapter 5, we noted that every collaborative effort we had studied had started from major conflict and crisis. In New Jersey, we wanted to develop a different, less traumatic path to collaboration.

The reasons that districts join the Collaborative are varied. Most similar efforts start with conferences and lectures, which generally produce a very low yield. In New Jersey, a key mechanism has been active recruitment of new districts by the State Support Group. This group, it will be recalled, includes leaders of the state unions and of the state associations of school boards, principals and supervisors, and superintendents. They are aware of which districts might be interested in trying a Collaborative Partnership and which are totally unready for such an effort. They also have long-term relationships and influence with district leaders. All of the early New Jersey cases, and many later ones, have come through this route.

Once there is some initial interest, we have found that the research evidence detailed in chapter 2—showing a strong link between collaboration and student achievement—is a powerful motivator. Many educators are attracted to the basic idea of collaboration, but they think of it mainly as a way to improve relations; to see that collaboration actually leads to improvements in student performance is something of a revelation. Many people have said to us, in effect, "That was the moment I was hooked!" Patrick Dolan, a consultant with long experience in this field, told us that he had

TABLE 8.1 Key elements of the interactive approach

1. Initial motivation/attraction	2. Operational foundations	3. Scaffolding and support	4. Research, assessment, review
State Support Group recommendations and influence	**Support structures** • District Leadership Teams • School Leadership Teams	**State Support Group** continuing guidance and influence	**Impacts of collaboration** (multiple outcomes)
Research on benefits to students and educators	**Improvement Initiatives**	**Capacity Building Workshops for districts** (5 days over 2–3 years)	**Culture/climate survey** (national calibration)
Interactive change approach (multi-stakeholder, web of support, action-focused)	**Collaborative process skills:** • problem-solving • decision-making • meeting management • project management • conflict resolution	**Learning networks:** Interdistrict and role-alike	**Deep dives:** e.g., • collaboration and COVID • collaboration and DEI • math versus ELA outcomes
Exposure to examples ("starter yeast") • national best practice examples • local New Jersey examples		**Peer Facilitators**	**Ongoing tracking of district progress** and self-study
Trust building		**Neutral convenor / facilitator**	
		Refresher workshops and ongoing support	
		Documents and tools as needed (document repository)	
		Professional Development and Executive Education	

always found the attraction of new participants to be a heavy lift. But, he told us, "your research evidence solves the problem of the heavy lift."

The multi-stakeholder approach, especially bringing together administrators, boards, and union leaders around the shared focus on improving student learning, may also be very attractive to some. They may have experienced one another as obstacles or even enemies; in any case, the difficulties in these relationships are often an unpleasant fact of life. The hope of actually working together can draw them into the effort.

The Collaborative has always put forward existing examples to give a sense of possibility. In the workshops, we have used materials on the ABC Unified School District in California, which has more than twenty-five years of experience of collaboration and has accumulated a trove of learnings. We have also used case studies from Montgomery, Maryland, and other districts. Increasingly, we have relied on the early district participants in the New Jersey effort, who can speak personally about their experiences. We call these presentations "starter yeast"—examples that can give new districts live examples of potential future expansion.

2. Operational Foundations

We have defined three core structural pieces on which collaboration is built: *collaborative leadership teams*, *improvement initiatives* for transforming teaching and learning, and common *process skills*.

Leadership Teams

The Collaborative's approach does not dismantle existing decision-making and governance structures in school boards, administration (superintendents, central office, principals, supervisors) or the union (president and executive board, building representatives). But it *adds* multi-stakeholder Leadership Teams, at the school and district level, responsible for overseeing the development of collaboration.[8]

The District Leadership Team (DLT) is chaired by the superintendent and the teacher union local president. The rest of the membership is flexible; it usually includes central office administrators, principals, supervisors, union executive board members or building representatives, and representatives of other groups as appropriate for the local circumstances. Similarly, the School Leadership Team (SLT), one in each school, includes the principal and a building union leader, supervisors, teachers, and other stakeholder representatives as needed.

These teams are responsible primarily for guiding the Collaborative effort. This means making sure that key stakeholder voices are heard, developing new structures and processes as needed, identifying problems, and commissioning improvement initiatives (more about that shortly). The teams are also typically involved in regular operations: for example, in many collaborative districts these teams had a major role in developing responses to the COVID-19 pandemic. As mentioned earlier, the scope of authority is not set in stone but continually develops; over time, effective Leadership Teams may take on a central role in the overall management of the distinct, but not all their decisions will be made by consensus.

Improvement Initiatives

Improvement initiatives embody the core principle of *action for improvement*— not just maintaining the system, but changing it for the better. Initiatives are conducted by Improvement Teams—a type of task force, commissioned by the Leadership Teams to work on particular projects for educational improvement. Improvement Teams are composed of people with interest and knowledge in that area, and they can disband when their work is done— which may take anywhere from a few weeks to several years, depending on the scope of the task. The team can also choose to take on a new initiative. They are crucial dynamic drivers of progress.

Improvement initiatives may vary widely. They have included—to take just a few examples at random—developing new instructional strategies; addressing student performance issues; creating peer mentoring systems for teachers; and developing support for diversity, equity, and inclusion efforts. In some schools of the Collaborative, as many as a third or more of teachers and staff are involved in leadership or initiative teams.

The Leadership Teams are responsible for approving and implementing the recommendations of initiative teams. Sometimes a Leadership Team takes on an initiative itself, especially in the early stages, but often, it defines the purpose and timeline and sets up a separate team to work on it. Thus, the initiative teams can cut across the system, drawing in new participants as needed from different levels and roles, including outside the district.

Collaborative Skills

Participants in most organizations are skilled in navigating bureaucratic requirements and structures. They are often less skilled in collaboration—working effectively with others when the hierarchy of control is not clear and the task can evolve over time. Thus, a foundational element of these efforts is the development of skills such as problem identification and selection, problem-solving, decision-making, meeting management, project management, and conflict resolution. Training in these skills has become fairly widespread in many industries during the last decade or two; we have adapted these tools to the public school environment.

Schools have another advantage over most organizations (in addition to a strong shared purpose): most of their employees are relatively good at these skills, since they work in generally collegial environments. But there are certainly exceptions, and even the best need development as they take on harder collaborative problems.

3. Scaffolding and Support

The past cases we reviewed in chapter 5 were heavily dependent on strong leaders, especially in their early phases. We have paid particular attention to developing a set of mechanisms that could support collaborative efforts from multiple directions, thus reducing this vulnerability. These include a regular set of Capacity Building Workshops, twice-yearly interdistrict meetings for mutual exchange and learning, a network of peer facilitators, some neutral convener/consultants, professional development opportunities, a set of reference documents and tools, and ongoing research. We touched on some of these briefly in the story of the New Jersey Collaborative; here we bring them together in a general model with wider applicability.

Capacity Building Workshops

Many participants' first connection to the Collaborative comes in initial district Capacity Building Workshops, designed in continuing discussions between the peer Facilitation Team and the Rutgers convener/consultants. In their current form, the workshops are a sequence of five days delivered in the first two to three years of operation. We call them *workshops* rather than using the more common term *training sessions* because they involve relatively little "training"—transfer of general concepts and skills—but a maximum of practice through work that participants directly apply to their own contexts.

In the first few years of any new Collaborative, these workshops need to be delivered by experienced outside convener/consultants. Later, as cohorts of peer facilitators are developed from within existing districts, they can take over considerable responsibility for leading the workshops. We will have much more to say later about these peer facilitators, who have become an essential ingredient in the growth and success of this process.

The workshops are constructed in modules that can be moved around according to districts' particular needs. They are largely composed of repeated building blocks:

- *conceptual inputs,* such as the structure of leadership teams or tools for problem-solving
- *opportunity for reflection and practice,* usually in facilitated breakout groups—often using simple diagnostic tools to assess the current state and working on applying the new tools
- *exercises*—team-building experiences

- *action planning*—developing specific plans for moving forward in the next phase, including plans for communicating with the rest of the district

A general principle is to introduce concepts and tools "just in time"—when the participants have *experienced* the need for them—and to follow immediately with practical reflection on those experiences, and with planning for improvement.

What follows is a *typical* sequence, though districts and facilitators may vary it as needed.

Day 1. The sequence starts with an overview of the research showing the connection of collaboration to student achievement and to teacher commitment and retention (see chapters 2–3). At the same time, the sequence introduces and develops the basic concepts of collaboration and partnership. Once peer facilitators have been identified—which usually takes a few years after entry into the Collaborative—they not only help lead workshops by presenting key concepts and action planning but also reflect about their experiences in developing their own collaborative systems.

A customization of a standard game theory negotiation exercise—the "Prisoner's Dilemma"—is used as a team-building activity. Participants are broken into teams that negotiate with one another and often end up undercutting one another to win. In one district, the union president and the superintendent led facing teams that double-crossed each other repeatedly. After general laughter and wry reflection, the two approached each other and "pinky swore" to change their relationship in the future.

Then the group works on two action plans: (1) developing initial plans for the creation of Leadership Teams at the district and school levels, and (2) defining some potential Improvement Initiatives and developing plans for finalizing and launching teams to work on them.

Day 2. In an ideal world, the second workshop day would follow immediately on the first; in the real world, we have found that most districts cannot free up people for two days in a row. So the second day is often held weeks or months later.

It starts with an approximately two-hour review of progress on the Leadership Teams and Improvement Initiatives. Next, we introduce a key set of problem-solving skills centered on two tools: the "Fishbone Diagram" for root cause analysis, and the Solutions Matrix for prioritizing potential solutions. Initial input is followed, as usual, by a chance to practice in breakout groups.[9]

We also introduce another exercise, "Desert Survival," with the objective of learning and practicing team-building skills and demonstrating the value of group decision-making.[10] By this time participants may already have experienced some disagreement about the decision rights of the various participants. So we follow with a model of decision-making rights: a five-step continuum from the extremes of decisions made solely by administration or union leadership to a central point of full consensus (described more fully in chapter 9).[11] We introduce criteria for choosing where a particular decision should be on that continuum, as well as processes for gradually moving more decisions toward the center and the Solutions Matrix for prioritizing potential solutions. An initial input is again followed by a chance to practice in breakout groups. The day closes with action planning for next steps and communication with the district at large.

Day 3. The third day is likely to be near the beginning of the second year. Since the summer's cobwebs need to be swept, more time than usual is allowed for initial self-diagnosis and review of progress. The main substantive inputs for the day are tools and worksheets on the management of meetings, including the use of agendas, definition of roles and responsibilities, shared documents, action planning, and review.

A major portion of the day is spent working on a mission statement. This task is left until this point in the expectation that by now districts will have encountered some practical difficulties and differences of views that need to be clarified. If the mission statement is done too early, it results in bromides that are not really put to use; if it comes too late, deep differences may fester. The leaders need to make a judgment call about when this discussion is appropriate and move other modules as needed.

An exercise, "The Pony," sparks discussion of effective listening and the challenge of working in teams. Whereas Desert Survival showed the benefit of working together, this exercise provides a complement by illustrating the difficulties.

As always, it is a priority for each team to have time for a facilitated breakout session for problem-solving and action planning.

Day 4. Day 4 is best held during the second half of the second year. In addition to the initial self-reflection and final action planning, this session has three key elements:

- The commissioning of new Improvement Initiatives. The conceptual inputs are a set of criteria and a worksheet (defining the purpose, stakeholders, timeline, and decision rights). This is followed by breakout sessions to apply these tools to existing and potential initiatives.
- A case study discussion of an example of collaborative reform. This is a way for participants to step back from their own experience and apply what they have learned to a different situation, which in turn helps to deepen their understanding of central concepts and tools.
- A module on project management for the Initiative Teams: how to plan the development of a project over time, set timelines, maintain accountability, work with important stakeholders outside the group, and build support.

The day closes as before with a period for action planning, with particular focus on how to communicate the work of the collaborative effort to the rest of the district.

Day 5. This session should be held early in the third year. The following are the main modules, beyond the usual self-reflection and action planning:

- An analysis of the partnership and changes in roles. Unionized teachers and administrative leaders meet separately to discuss their own assessment of how the partnership is working and then come together for an exchange of views and a discussion of how to improve.
- A discussion of engaging new stakeholders. By this time, the collaborative effort should be ready to consider involving new parties such as the school board, parents, students, and non-teaching staff. The peer facilitators review their own experiences in stretching the boundaries of involvement, and the workshop participants discuss potential next steps for their district(s).

Again, this curriculum should be thought of as a set of modules to be delivered, as much as possible, at the time when districts see the need for them. The modules can be moved around to address the "hot" issues of the moment.

Interdistrict and Role-Alike Networks

We continue now with the elements of "scaffolding and support" for the collaborative effort, as listed earlier in table 8.1.

The Capacity Building Workshop sessions are not usually sufficient by themselves to keep the districts moving and developing their Collaborative Partnerships. A second major piece is the *Interdistrict Learning Network meetings*, held twice a year. In these sessions, large numbers of districts and people—we have had up to 370 people at a time—can hear about some of the leading-edge challenges and potential of collaboration. Sometimes they meet in small groups with people from other districts around common problems. Some sessions also include "role-alike" discussions, in which superintendents, union leaders, board members, principals, and those in other roles meet separately to share their common experiences and ideas.

There is usually time for districts to meet separately, so participants can spend some time with people in their own districts, whom they don't see regularly, to reflect on how they can use what they've heard.

These sessions often give a large boost in momentum and introduce new ideas to the districts. Seeing other similar schools struggling with the same problems and hearing how those schools have dealt with their problems give the participants a sense of possibility, transcending the frustrations that almost always develop, and help them see beyond the grooves that are worn more deeply over time in any system. Participants also find resources in other districts that they follow up with after the meeting, further deepening the idea of a "learning network."

State-Level Support Group

The role of the State Support Group (composed of leaders of state associations and other stakeholders) has evolved as the Collaborative has matured. The members now do less recruitment of new districts. (Some of this task passes to the peer network: new districts hear about the effort from their colleagues, then come to learning network meetings before committing.) Members of the state-level team have increasingly focused on troubleshooting in cases of conflict, working with their members to find ways through the difficulties and to reinforce the principles of the Collaborative. More recently, they have helped in establishing links with their national associations, which is becoming increasingly important as interest in the Collaborative spreads beyond New Jersey.

There have been no representatives of state government on this team. This was initially an accident of political conditions in the state. But as we will discuss later, we do believe it is important to collaborate actively with political officials as major stakeholders.

Peer Facilitators

The "web of support" is further strengthened through the development of a network/team of peer facilitators. These are leaders with significant experience in existing collaborative districts. In New Jersey, they have included superintendents, local union presidents and building representatives, principals, supervisors, teachers, and school board members.

Candidates should ordinarily have been working at least two years in a collaborative district, and should attend an initial facilitator training session of two to three days. These sessions are more like training than workshops, with more emphasis on content and skills. The entire group of facilitators also meets for two to three days every year to discuss what they have learned and to develop approaches to the leading-edge challenges they face.

The peer facilitators have turned out to be another innovation whose power we did not fully appreciate at the start. The benefits are varied and substantial. As peer educators, the facilitators have immediate credibility because they understand the system in depth and have struggled with similar problems. They benefit as well by broadening their experience, and their own districts benefit from their increased leadership skill. When there is resistance from one stakeholder in a district, as almost always happens at some point, a facilitator from another district with the same role—a board member, a superintendent, a union leader, a principal, and so on—can offer better help and build more influence than any outside consultant. The facilitators learn from one another and have contributed significantly to the improvement of the curriculum and the practice.

Other attempts at systemic change we have studied have been weakened by overreliance on outside consultants: costs were high and did not decrease with scale, and the interests of the outsiders were not fully aligned with the schools.[12] Both of these problems are greatly reduced by the use of peer facilitators. As they learn, they are able to take on many tasks and to bring costs down with increasing scale, and they are deeply embedded in the system they are working to reform.

Neutral Convener/Consultants

We have noted that an overdependence on outside consultants has often weakened reform efforts—both by increasing expenses and by diminishing the internal commitments necessary to sustain change in the long run. But that does not mean that outside experts are completely unnecessary: they play some important roles. Our approach has been to define a role for outside consultants that is relatively minimal and focused on the functions that they do best, while developing the peer support network as quickly as possible.

First, outsiders are generally needed as neutral conveners for the multi-stakeholder State Support Group. Convening this team cannot be done by any one of the stakeholder groups: the whole effort would quickly become unbalanced, and trust would be undermined. Even when relations have stabilized, a neutral party can be important in helping manage conflicts.

Second, there is a need for expert knowledge of organizational change and development. The State Support Group provides general guidance and direction, but they are not equipped to do the detailed work of development of networks and curricula. The peer facilitators can gradually take on more of this role, but they, too, come from different stakeholders and benefit from a neutral reference point.

Third, as mentioned earlier, outsiders can act as catalysts. Since they have a broad overview of the field and the history of many efforts, they can often bring forward issues and patterns that have not yet become apparent to the day-to-day participants and may help overcome obstacles or move to new levels of innovation.

Fourth, outsiders can conduct research within and across efforts, to establish benchmarks, show the impact, identify potential trouble spots, and assess the effectiveness of innovations.

In New Jersey, these functions were taken by the Collaborative School Leadership Initiative at Rutgers, which performed a variety of functions:

- It hosted the initial meeting of the people that became the State Support Group and coordinated its meetings and agendas over many years.
- It led the Capacity Building Workshops for a number of years, gradually sharing the role with the peer facilitators.

- It organized the first interdistrict meetings, again moving increasing responsibility to the peer leaders over time.
- It has led yearly facilitator training and review sessions to focus on new skills and to crystallize learnings.
- It has codified these learnings into a curriculum, with much input from the Facilitation Team, and gathered informational documents in a repository that can be easily accessed by participants as needed.
- It has helped establish learning links through conferences involving national exemplars such as the ABC Unified School District.
- It has conducted ongoing research both within New Jersey and beyond as a way to benchmark progress and assess the effectiveness of collaboration.

A university is in general a good base for these roles, since it is not aligned with any stakeholder and usually has less profit pressure than consulting firms; but some independent nonprofit groups, such as the Consortium for Educational Change and the California Labor Management Initiative, have also had success.

"Refresher" Workshops and Continued Support (as Needed)

The support system goes through three main phases:

- Phase 1 includes the first three years. The five days of workshops described earlier are delivered in this phase. We also offer support from peer facilitators as needed: the peer facilitators divide into pairs (with representatives of union and management), covering two to three districts each. They are generally available for two to four days a year in each district.
- Phase 2 covers years 4–5. The regular workshops described earlier are finished, but most districts are still developing and expanding their ambitions. The interdistrict network meetings offer space for reflection and further learning. In addition, follow-up one-day

workshops may be designed as needed to cover concepts and tools
that need to be deepened or extended.

- Phase 3, starting with the sixth year, should need less support.
Generally the two days of interdistrict meetings are enough. By this
time, moreover, many districts will have representatives in the peer
facilitator network who can help lead the internal efforts. Some continued support from the peer facilitators or additional workshops
are still available for districts in need.

As the districts grow more mature, they can define their own needs and
reach out to the facilitators or their peers in the interdistrict and role-alike
networks.

Documents and Tools (Document Repository)

A set of materials coordinated with the main Capacity Building Workshop
topics is available to all participants. Having the material online in a docu-
ment repository enables us to keep materials up to date and to respond to
new demands. It is often very helpful to include materials invented by the
districts themselves, as they try out variants of the basic structures and processes, as well as take on new improvement challenges.

The expectation is that district participants will dip into the repository
when they have a particular problem or a need for clarification. It is therefore important that it be easy to navigate, so people can go quickly to what
they are looking for. Just a few key documents or worksheets are needed
for each topic, perhaps along with background readings for those who want
to go deeper.

Professional Development and Executive Education

Typically the professional development opportunities in public schools have
nothing to do with collaboration or systems change. Sometimes they run
in the opposite direction: board members are taught to stay at arm's length

to preserve their negotiating positions, and union officials are taught hard bargaining. There is little thought to teaching the issues and role changes involved in collaboration.

An important function of the State Support Group members is to develop new materials in the educational offerings of their own associations. The Rutgers Center for Collaborative School Leadership has also developed an executive education program at Rutgers. Modules for regular Professional Development days in the schools are also under development.

4. Research, Assessment, Review

The last major pillar for collaboration consists of mechanisms for research, assessment, and review. This is an aspect of organizational change that is too often neglected: people try things and then keep moving, without enough evidence of what worked and what did not, and without reflecting and drawing lessons for application the next time. Stopping to look back feels like a distraction when you are charging forward; but it is, however, an essential element of successful development.

One vital element in the research-assessment-review piece of the model is formal research that can be calibrated against broad national or state samples. Sometimes, the most successful efforts generate the most dissatisfaction because they raise hopes and expectations; benchmarking progress against others can be very encouraging. Conversely, districts may become complacent if they feel good, even if they're not making much actual progress. A Rutgers/Cornell survey was used as the basis for much of the research in chapters 2–3, and has been the main comparative tool in New Jersey, but there are others as well. The most useful of these measure the impact of collaboration on important outcomes such as student achievement and teacher turnover.

"Deep dives" into particular issues of the moment are also valuable. Recently, for example, we have been focusing on the impact of collaboration on schools' responses to the COVID-19 pandemic. Graduate students are generally delighted at the opportunity to explore such topics.

Finally, it is important to keep track of progress. Without deliberate effort, it is impossible to follow the range of initiatives and innovations under way in the participating districts or to spot early signs of trouble. A short annual survey asking for basic information on the functioning of the Leadership Teams and the progress of Improvement Initiatives provides data for distributing the Collaborative's resources and spotting emerging issues.

SEQUENCE OF STEPS

Boiling this down to its essence, here is a short summary of steps for key leaders in a collaborative reform effort.

For the State Support Group

FIRST:

- Bring together state association leaders: boards of education, unions, superintendents, principals, and other key stakeholders plus a neutral convener/consultant.
- Identify districts for three to four pilot efforts.
- Support the development of curriculum and an initial set of workshops.

AFTER ONE TO TWO YEARS:

- Sponsor interdistrict meetings.
- Identify candidates for peer facilitators and sponsor training.
- Invite new districts.

AFTER THREE TO FOUR YEARS:

- Develop ongoing network meetings: interdistrict and role-alike.
- Support evaluation and research.

For District Leaders

1. Gain initial commitment by school board, union, and management leaders.
2. Participate in one to two days of initial training, including district leaders, union-management teams, and teachers from selected schools.
3. Start District Leadership Teams, School Leadership Teams, and some initial Improvement Initiatives.
4. Organize participants for follow-up workshops in the first three years.
5. Attend interdistrict and role-alike network sessions.
6. Identify internal facilitator candidates after two to three years.
7. Seek support from follow-up workshops, peer facilitators, and other members of the network as needed.

Organic Scaling

A major difficulty for any organization change is moving to scale. It is relatively easy to work informally and adaptively in a small group, but it is usually assumed that as a project grows bigger, it needs to become more standardized. This is one reason for the common tendency toward a top-down "programmatic" model of change, despite the considerable evidence of its ineffectiveness.

In certain respects, standardization is valuable. We have certainly learned from the many experiments in collaborative change over decades, including the New Jersey effort as well as others described earlier in this book. Many of these lessons, positive and negative, do not need to be relearned and can be incorporated into standardized processes. At the same time, there is undoubtedly much still to be learned in the future, new challenges to address, and innovations to try. So we need—as suggested early in this chapter—a model of change that combines programmatic with participatory aspects (or, in language used in recent decades, a diagnostic with a dialogic approach).[13]

An important study of a major "comprehensive school reform" effort of the 1990s provides some of the best evidence in support of an approach that combines central coordination with decentralized learning.[14] It showed, first, that programs driven strongly from the outside have short life spans: schools in the initial phase that depended heavily on outside funding and intervention did well for a few years but faded quickly when the support decreased. Second, it showed that programs that are built from inside are more durable: other districts that picked up aspects of the method on their own and developed their own sources of funding lasted much longer. Finally, it showed the need for ongoing central coordination: the most successful cases remained scattered and isolated, with no mechanisms for sharing learning or developing improved methods from experience, so the effort never achieved systemic scale or impact.

The model described in this chapter aims to combine decentralized development and learning with large-scale coordination. The model has been successful so far at both innovation and growth. It is built primarily through the efforts of the participants, learning as they go and adapting the approach to their own situations. This leads to strong rootedness in daily work and relations, and generates a self-perpetuating virtuous circle in which the participating districts can turn for support to one another and to knowledgeable peer facilitators from similar locales. The peer facilitators have very high credibility with new districts, since they have been through the same process themselves, starting in roughly the same place. At the same time, the model provides methods for sharing among districts through interdistrict meetings, role-alike networks, and annual meetings of the peer Facilitation Team. Problems can be addressed as they arise in individual districts by the peer facilitators and in network meetings when problems emerge across multiple districts. Finally, broadly applicable learnings can be incorporated in the initial workshops and guidelines for new districts, enriching a standardized core for the effort that improves over time.

It should again be noted that this is also a very *inexpensive* method of scaling: there is very little administrative overhead, and the peer facilitators are paid at rates less than the inflated rates of outside consulting firms. A great deal of learning happens through mutually beneficial exchanges rather than formal, high-cost training programs.

Although the New Jersey Collaborative is probably the largest collaborative school network in the country—as of this writing, it involves twenty-five districts—it is a very long way from making a major impact on the state or the nation as a whole. Can it be scaled to thousands of districts at a feasible cost?

There is no logistical reason why the process used to grow so far cannot continue to expand. There are some limitations to the size of peer networks: interdistrict meetings, with their high degree of discussion and teamwork, can't really be managed beyond a few hundred people, and peer relationships are best formed within relatively defined communities. So we expect that we will begin to "chunk" the effort into distinct networks of about twenty-five to fifty districts each, with their own sets of peer facilitators and interdistrict learning sessions. That will require another level of support to coordinate across the networks. But again, this support can be very light, focused essentially on establishing a system-wide knowledge-sharing platform and occasional meetings to cross-fertilize the major developments. As part of this effort, we have begun to build role-alike support networks of school board members, superintendents, union leaders, and principals.

We have considered two other issues in future scaling:

Pacing. Since this is conceived as an organic process—building trust through experience, growing largely from the work of district and school participants, and adapting to varying conditions in each state and region— further scaling in new states should *begin* relatively slowly, increasing speed after the initial relationships solidify. The scaling might proceed as follows:

- A State Support Group would recruit approximately five to ten districts per year for the first five years.

- A small nucleus of neutral outsider conveners would run the initial workshops, building up a solid cohort of districts working through the problems of building trust and capacity.
- Interdistrict meetings would start about the second year, when there were enough districts and enough experience to make them meaningful.
- In the third and fourth years, the Collaborative would identify natural leaders emerging from all the stakeholders as potential peer facilitators and hold the first facilitator workshops. Facilitator training could be combined across states for economies of scale, as could exemplars from early adopting states that could serve as "incubators" or "labs" to help new states build capacity.
- After that, the pace could pick up, increasing by a third each year to the number of existing districts. At that rate, the effort could reach all of the districts in most states in about ten more years.
- Outside consultants would continue to have an important role as neutral conveners and coordinators, but they would be a very small part of the effort. We calculate that under the assumptions listed here, only two full-time outsiders would be needed for three hundred to five hundred districts. This factor by itself dramatically reduces cost.

Cost: Using the basic elements above, we have developed a model that could be scaled at a reasonable cost. The assumptions include:

- five days of workshops for all incoming districts over the first three years, and one more day available in the following two years
- four to five days a year of follow-up facilitation in the districts, by peer facilitators and outside convener/consultants, for the first three years, and two to three days per year for the next two years

- one to two days of workshops or follow-up facilitation available per year for districts after the first five years, as needed
- two days of Interdistrict Learning Network Conference sessions per year available to all districts (for as many people as they want to bring)
- sufficient peer facilitators to cover these requirements, with each individual using no more than nine days per year during the school year
- two days per year of training workshops for peer facilitators (to be held in summer)
- sufficient convener/consultants to cover these requirements
- basic administrative support and web page maintenance

For this model, the overall cost is minuscule compared to other efforts of the kind. A report from the University of Michigan's Population Health Institute shows that prior programs for "comprehensive school reform" have cost from $100,000 to $284,000 *per school* in the first year; that is clearly a heavy burden, requiring significant outside financing.[15] By contrast, the cost of the organic model we have proposed is $10,000–$15,000 per year for each *district*. This is well below the cost of most Professional Development or curricular programs being adopted by districts around the country. It is financially feasible and sustainable with current resources on a system-wide scale.

CONCLUSION

This model of reform has developed from a great deal of experience and experimentation both within the New Jersey Collaborative and across all the efforts described in earlier chapters. It has demonstrated remarkable strength over the past decade, as shown by the fact that nearly all the districts that have begun the process are still actively engaged in it.

The learning is not finished, of course. There are issues at the leading edge that we are still exploring, such as more direct involvement of parents and the appropriate role of school boards. And if the model continues to grow, it will face challenges in involving new stakeholders across states and at the national level. We will discuss these issues further in the next chapter.

But the core structures and processes are now well developed. There is good evidence, both from our research and from the New Jersey experience, that Collaborative Partnership is a robust model that could reach sufficient scale to serve as an alternative to the policies of recent decades.

CHAPTER 9

Collaboration in Action

PATHS OF DEVELOPMENT AND CRITICAL MOMENTS

WHILE GENERAL MODELS like those described in chapter 8 are important, they don't capture what it's like to *experience* the move toward collaboration. They are like showing an explorer's journey on a small-scale map—ignoring the detours, the mountains and chasms crossed, the periods of slow and rapid movement, the moments of enthusiasm and despair. In this chapter, we return to some experiences of the districts of the New Jersey Collaborative—particularly the longest-running ones—to fill in the living story.

COMMON OBSTACLES

We'll start with two of the most common obstacles in the early phases of the collaborative process.

The Problem of Time

The first concern of participants is almost always, "Where can we find the time for extra collaborative meetings? We're already drowning in things we have to do." The lack of time seems to many an insurmountable obstacle. It often becomes an initial focus of discussion in the Leadership Teams.

Some have even commissioned special project teams to explore new ideas to find time.

Yet we rarely hear this concern after the first year. The solution is not some dramatic revelation or new mechanism; rather, the collaborative systems gradually work their way into daily practice, and after a time people have trouble remembering what the changes were.

In general, there seem to be several major ways in which time is found:

- Some bits of extra time can almost always be created through scheduling changes. This has included the use of common periods set aside for class preparation, especially for members of project teams, and adjusting schedules to free time slots for members of Leadership Teams.
- As one teacher commented with a wry smile, "You can take existing meetings and make them more efficient." Every organization has time spent in unproductive ways that can be identified and repurposed. Professional Development (PD) periods, for example, are often seen by teachers as of limited use; several districts have involved teachers in adapting some of these PD sessions to advance collaborative skills and projects. Faculty meetings have been compressed to leave time for project teams to get together. Another time sink has almost disappeared in many collaborative districts: grievances, which typically take considerable time for all the people usually involved in paperwork, oversight, and argumentation.
- Implementation of many outside mandates is greatly speeded up, because by the time decisions are worked through collaboratively, those responsible for implementing them both understand the rationale and support the approach. This has been most broadly visible in responses to the COVID-19 pandemic, which sparked intense conflict in many districts; but as we will detail later in this chapter, the Collaborative's districts reached solutions that were implemented rapidly and with little resistance.

"If it's important enough," a union official commented, "people will find time for it. The key point is that people need to be convinced this is not a waste of their time. That was years in the making, convincing people that their involvement will actually make a difference. Now we've reached a point where they say, 'This is a great use of our time.'"

Over time, as shown by the cases in chapter 5, the "extra" meetings and discussions become regular parts of a new *system* of rich interactions, which greatly reduces friction—conflicts, misunderstandings, resistances—and thus operates far more efficiently.

Decision Rights

Another issue of concern for many entering into collaborative relations is: Who gets to make final decisions? Does this mean that superintendents and principals can't decide anything? Does it mean we ignore the contract and just try to get along?

The answer to these questions, of course, is no; but it's a complicated no. We stress from the first Capacity Building Workshop the danger of "pseudo-collaboration": pretending to collaborate when in reality a decision has already been made. But that doesn't answer the question of what the limits of collaboration really are.

Clearly, collaboration does not mean that all decisions are made by consensus: no organization could function on that basis. Some decisions are driven by policies from forces outside the Collaborative, such as government mandates. Some are too pressing for full discussion, and some are just not worth the time. There are also decisions on which one group—sometimes teachers, sometimes technical staff, sometimes administrators—have far more knowledge than others; their voice should be privileged.

But the real key is that collaborative decision-making is not a matter of formal rights, but rather a gradual process of trust-building. In a collaborative effort, trust is built through the many experiences of working with other parties. In early phases, those who hold responsibility are typically cautious about letting go; but over time, if collaboration works well, trust grows that all parties really have the interests of students at heart and the competence to make good decisions. Thus, more decisions gradually become more collaborative, and power is more rarely used.

One of the early districts encountered this problem in one of its first major improvement initiatives. For many years, teachers had made recommendations to the administration about changing the school year calendar. When the Collaborative was introduced, a committee of volunteers was formed and took it upon themselves to improve the calendar. With great enthusiasm they developed a new calendar on their own, not realizing it was a school board prerogative. When the school board rejected their recommendation over a variety of concerns including contract violations, PD, teaching days, and so on, all of the stakeholders—teachers, administration, union, and board—were upset. This naturally led to a crisis of trust: administrators and the board were accused of "pseudo-collaboration." But it also became clear to all that this topic was not a good one for starting the process of collaboration in the district because the authority to make this rested solely with the board. Shortly thereafter, at one of the workshops, participants learned of the "decision-making continuum," described in chapter 8, which had been used in previous efforts to distinguish decisions that rest solely with one party (administration or union) from decisions on which there is consultation and ones that can be made entirely by consensus (table 9.1).

By clarifying expectations, this continuum helped defuse tensions. But as a participant put it years later, it just "kicked the can down the road": now the question was, Who gets to decide where on the continuum this decision falls? In the case of the calendar proposal, it was clear that the school board had legal power and responsibility. But what about decisions involving the leaders within the Collaborative: the superintendent, union officials, principals, and so on? Did they just get to say when their authority trumped that of the other stakeholders?

TABLE 9.1 The continuum of shared decision-making

1	2	3	4	5
		Shared/Collaborative		
Administrator-centered	Consultative	Consensual	Consultative	Staff-centered
Administration decision (without staff input), and staff will be informed: "administration will tell staff."	Administration decision, on which staff consult: "staff gives input, then administration makes the final decision."	Equal weight decision: "we made the final decision together"	Staff decision, with input from administration: "administration gives staff input, but staff makes the final decision"	Staff decision (within administration guidelines), and staff will inform administration: "staff will tell administration."

In discussions of these questions with the participants and the peer facilitators, four criteria emerged as a basis for decisions about the continuum:

- the urgency of the decision (urgent decisions allow less time for collaboration)
- whether the decision involves mandates, regulations, or legal requirements, so that those responsible for implementing requirements from outside the Collaborative have ultimate decision rights
- whether the decision requires specialized expertise or tacit knowledge (people with specialized knowledge should have added weight in decision-making)
- whose support is needed for implementation (those whose support is needed should understand and support the decision)

This, by the way, is one of many examples of a tool adopted in one district that was later incorporated by the peer facilitators into the basic curriculum. In difficult cases, these criteria can be the basis for discussion about where the decision falls on the continuum.

Over the next few years, the Leadership Teams tinkered with the continuum, at one point drawing it as a circle rather than a two-ended line. They explored the area between the extremes of unilateral and consensus decisions—the areas of consultation and discussion. And they found that even if the *what* of a decision was not open for discussion, the *how* of implementation could benefit from collaboration.

It became clear over time that most decisions fall in a gray area, where one party may have formal rights but chooses not to assert them because that party finds benefit in collaboration—having seen that the process leads to greater engagement and support for decisions and that new voices are heard and new ideas surfaced, so that decisions are in the end better, easier to implement, and accepted as fair.

So now the struggle in this district and others becomes: How can we maximize involvement without abandoning legal responsibilities?

At this point, *trust* moves to the center. As parties with power believe that the others are acting in good faith to advance teaching and learning, they are increasingly willing to relax their assertions of right. One superintendent described his evolution:

> There was a time in the beginning where I felt that the work that we started to do through the Collaborative might be a little bit rocky. And I used to think of the graph of how you meet in the middle with some scales two, three, four. And I felt we'd be at one [i.e., unilateral decisions] all the time. But as we got to know each other and started to develop a sense of respect, the respect came from purposeful communication.

In essence, when this works, participants learn that decision *rights* are not the only issue. If parties insist on their rights, taking a large proportion of decisions out of the collaborative process, the collaboration will die. But when there are visible benefits in sharing power, the parties explore how far they can trust one another to make decisions in the common interest. It becomes increasingly rare for one party to assert prerogatives and override the collaborative process; more decisions in practice approach the central point of consensus.

The Development of Improvement Initiatives

The initial workshop encourages districts to start with relatively easy Improvement Initiatives—ones that are largely within their control and could reasonably be accomplished within a year. At the school level, a few of these have had to do with "climate" issues, such as improving morale. But in keeping with the emphasis on improving teaching and learning, many districts took on more difficult educational issues, especially ones that teachers could influence directly, such as student performance, homework policies, sharing instructional practices, or improving communication with parents. After a year or two of learning, they began work on more complicated initiatives involving multiple parts of a school, such as organizing interdepartmental teams for teaching or choosing among competing web platforms for learning. At the district level, successful early projects have included curriculum revisions, tech planning, and standardizing report cards.

In a few cases, as in the calendar example discussed earlier, the teams took on issues that were too ambitious—outside their scope of knowledge and power. This proved initially discouraging, but discussion in interdistrict meetings and other venues led to the clarification of the decision-making criteria and issues, giving new impetus to the effort.

A central goal of the Collaborative is for schools and districts to develop the capabilities for complex and long-term projects for transforming fundamental elements of the school system. This involves many aspects, such as the following:

- a general understanding among all parties about what is commonly called "systems improvement," including establishing roles and responsibilities of participants, project management, planning steps and milestones, holding one another accountable, making effective use of expertise, and problem-solving skills
- building a high level of trust among parties who have not worked together in the past or who have had adversarial relations
- building support among outside parties who will need to be involved in final decision-making and implementation

Those skills are not usually widely present at the start. Most teachers work largely autonomously in their own classrooms. Most administrators and union officials are used to performing specified roles and defending their turf against interference. Not many are good at the give-and-take of collaboration, at building trust through listening and showing openness and vulnerability, or at understanding the mechanics of managing a multidisciplinary team. As one principal put it,

I was really taken with some of the data. And I remember to this day very clearly a particular slide that talked about principals who work collaboratively are seen more as a resource. And that was counterintuitive to me at the time. I was a fairly new principal and I was pretty sure that I was hired because I had good ideas, was a good problem solver, and I was a good building manager and instructional leader—and that I could do a lot of things *for* teachers. I didn't really think about doing a lot of things *with* teachers. But that slide said the more decisions I share with teachers, the more of a resource they will see me as—it really almost knocked me off my chair to think of it that way. It certainly makes sense. We've always talked about the importance of building teacher leaders and distributed leadership. But I don't know that I was really practicing that.

His union counterpart confirms the principal's account.

Beyond this example, the range of initiatives across the districts has been impressive. Collaborative teams have made significant improvements in Professional Development, curriculum planning, technology choices, peer mentoring among teachers, grading systems, homework policies, and many other issues central to the success of students.

THE DEVELOPMENT OF LEADERSHIP TEAMS

Workshops for the early districts gave only general guidelines for the overall structure of the Leadership Teams at the district and school levels. Figure 9.1 presents the model shown in those workshops (U = union leader; M = administration leader).

But as they matured and took on more complex problems, districts developed their own variants to manage all the stakeholder connections. One district, after seven years, developed a structure like the one shown in figure 9.2.

The superintendent of this district explained:

School Leadership Teams in all of our schools consist of a leadership triad: a principal, the head building representative, and a teacher. Our District

FIGURE 9.1   An early model of Leadership Team structures

Governance

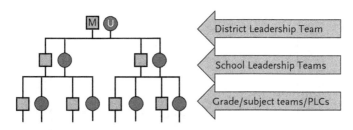

Leadership Team consists of district administrators, union members and teacher leaders.

We focus on curriculum, instruction, and student services across the continuum. Each school leadership team really does produce the lion's share of the outputs, which are to establish compelling learning expectations for kids and for teachers. Their role is to align curriculum in order to support teachers as a way to empower students. Their functions are:

- to collect data and analyze it as it relates to student learning and as it relates to local and high stakes assessments; establish vertical and horizontal structures to listen;
- to learn, to share and to connect with the DLT;
- to communicate learning and challenges to the school community; to identify conditions for school environment;
- to focus on student learning;
- to implement strategies that support students that support staff and families.

This is a collaboratively developed job description of a School Leadership Team. They're committed to each other, they're committed to collaborate, and they're committed to the development and enhancement of a culture that supports that. Their role really is to listen and learn from the folks they represent on the front lines and from each other. And

FIGURE 9.2 One district's Leadership Team structure after seven years

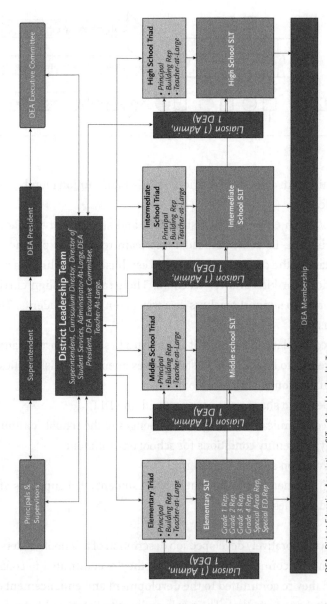

DEA = District Education Association;, SLT = School Leadership Team

Source: Dr. David Fitzgibbon, "Shaping Our Buildings: A Case Study of Organizational Learning in a Collaborative School District," EdD dissertation, Saint Peter's University, 2022.

it's a non-negotiable that those who are on our SLTs actively engage in that process.

A particularly important feature of the diagram in figure 9.2 are the multiple feedback loops and links. The various two-headed arrows represent real dialogues, not just formal approval processes. The leaders emphasize the role of the "liaisons," district-level administrators and union officials who serve as links between the District and School Leadership Teams:

> The liaisons helped to build the capacity for the School Leadership Teams. They helped to prevent "pseudo-collaboration" by guiding the school teams on the basic tenets of collaboration and getting alignment on expectations. That way the school teams didn't go off on projects without understanding the obstacles faced at the district level. But they could push back—ask for clarification, push for alignment of words with actions from the district leaders. The liaisons don't tell the SLTs what to do or not do. They provide information and communication links.

And to top it off!

> We also have another form of staff feedback called full staff feedback loops. It probably happens two or three times a year over a major initiative where the School Leadership Team really does need some direction on a particular issue from the full staff. So the intent behind the feedback loops is to afford every single member of the faculty the ability to contribute to solutions.

Another district drew its structure as shown in figure 9.3. Here it is notable that the structure includes a broad array of stakeholders, including paraprofessionals, custodians, parents, nurses, and students. It also directs attention to forces above the district administration, such as the board of education and "Trenton"—referring to the state government and Department of Education. And some of these have already been brought

FIGURE 9.3 Another district's Leadership Team structure after seven years

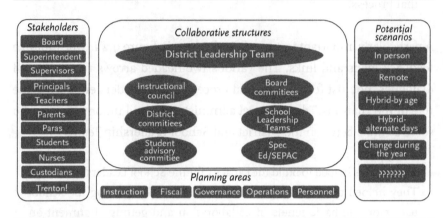

Source: Facilitation Team slide.

into the formal collaborative structure, at least to some extent. "SEPAC" is a parents' group concerned with special education; and board subcommittees now meet twice a year with collaborative initiative teams in their areas of responsibility for interactive discussions.

Drilling down into the internal structure of the teams, we find a similar variety. The District Leadership Teams often begin with union and administrative leaders and then bring in others. Many mature DLTs have representatives from each school, and some from other major functions, such as curriculum development. At least one now includes a board member as a regular attendee.

The School Leadership Teams, similarly, tend to start with the principal and a union building leader and then grows more complex. A high school principal described the SLT after seven years:

> We have nine teachers from different disciplines or departments, a secretary, a paraprofessional and a school nurse along with the principal, me, a vice principal and some content area supervisors. The team was mutually selected by our head union rep from our building and me sitting down to discuss who we felt best met the needs of our school and who could

work well together and get a great representation from our school body. We decided that we would meet monthly during the school day and give all of our members the same prep period.

Another long-standing School Leadership Team commissioned a set of Improvement Initiatives as satellites of the team, as shown in figure 9.4. They began with the "Solutions" satellite, focused on maintenance tasks— the (relatively) small problems that crop in everyday operation and that make work more difficult and unpleasant, such as dress codes, substitute teacher shortages, testing schedules, safety drills, attendance procedures, technology protocols, and student behavior issues in the lunchroom and hallways. These initial successes established the credibility for the effort and attracted a great deal of interest throughout the school. Then they took on more ambitious projects involving significant shifts in the school's operations, commissioning special improvement initiatives that included one member of the main School Leadership Team and a set of other relevant stakeholders. At the stage pictured in figure 9.4, nearly half of the school's teachers were working on one or more of these teams.

FIGURE 9.4   A School Leadership Team's structure with satellite Improvement Initiatives

Source: Facilitation Team slide.

VARIANT TRAJECTORIES

Collaborative districts have taken very different routes. A few cases are worth describing briefly. In one, the union was largely skeptical from early in the process, and trust between the union and the administration was low. The two parties tangled often over decision rights. Nevertheless, with the backing of many administrators and union members, there was considerable progress in a number of the schools and some district initiatives. After four years of this situation, a new union election led to an overwhelming victory for a new union team strongly committed to the Collaborative.

In a second case, the main problem lay with the board of education: several key members were actively opposed to partnership with the union. The superintendent was verbally supportive but, caught in the political crossfire, did little to encourage the effort. For about four years, the load was carried primarily by two schools with very active School Leadership Teams. Changes in union leadership and superintendents increased support from those stakeholders. Finally, a school board election returned a strong majority in favor of good union-management relations and the Collaborative; the new board president rapidly became an active advocate and participant.

In a third case, the Collaborative made a strong start with full support from both the union and administration but, after two years, hit a "plateau": there was a sense of confusion and stasis, and improvement initiatives were making little headway. After two retreats, and in discussions at interdistrict meetings, the leaders clarified the format for School Leadership Teams and the process for defining and deciding on improvement initiatives. This helped reenergize the effort.

There have been many other instances in which districts have gone through periods of struggle and frustration but have emerged with renewed energy. As one peer facilitator put it, "It's when you go through the sandy patches, the difficult moments, that you often learn the most."

These stories, along with many others, demonstrate a crucial point: the multiplicity of levels and stakeholders in the collaborative process often serves to stabilize it; when one party turns cold or even hostile, others can keep it going. The "scaffolding" mechanisms described in chapter 8—the workshops, inter-district meetings, peer facilitators, and so on—have developed many points of support. And so far at least, the record in New Jersey has been that almost all the districts that have started the process have had champions at multiple levels who kept developing relations and trust, and eventually others were drawn in.

MEETING STRATEGIC CHALLENGES

As collaborative attitudes and skills are developed, some schools and districts have developed capabilities for taking on complex and long-term projects for transforming fundamental aspects of the system.

The COVID-19 Crisis

The districts of the Collaborative—both more mature districts and some of the newer ones as well—proved their effectiveness in dealing with the greatest systemic challenge of the years 2020–22: the COVID-19 pandemic, still not fully resolved at the time of this writing. COVID presented schools and school districts with an unprecedented set of complexities through which swirled issues of the health and safety for students and teachers, childcare coverage dilemmas for working parents, lack of knowledge of causes and effects of the new disease, and uncertainty about the effectiveness of safety measures—all in an environment poisoned by the politicization of the crisis. Many districts in the state collapsed into open conflict, with administrators, parents, and teachers making conflicting demands with escalating intensity, sometimes ending in the courtroom or the picket lines.

The structures, processes, and mindset of the school districts participating in the New Jersey Collaborative were tested to their limits. "This has been a challenging year and a half, no question about it," said one state union leader. "But I would argue that as a result of our collaboration, we are stronger together and we have been able to navigate through the pandemic in very different ways than we might have prior to our work together."

A superintendent in one of the first districts in the Collaborative described the district's process:

> We developed a hybrid calendar in the summer, and we stuck with that the whole year. We didn't have closures. We even moved the end of the year up early and started the '21–'22 school year, in collaboration with the union, as late as possible, to get the longest summer that I've ever had in my decades in education. We agreed with the association to do September as all remote for most students, except for the youngest and most vulnerable.
>
> Collaborative decisions were made for the cleaning protocols, ventilation levels, building densification, entry procedures in and out of the buildings, temperature checks, etc. We welcomed in the union's industrial hygienists and we made them part of our meetings. And we changed some policies: for example, we expanded the opportunity for full-year leaves to non-tenured as well as tenured teachers.
>
> In the midst of all this, we were able to settle a very favorable contract for the union, and the rank-and-file members were really, really thrilled with this.
>
> So we're really proud of the existing structures that were in place that allowed us to continue on this path. It would have been really easy for the teachers to say we're disgusted, for the board to say we're going to just put this on hold and let the expired contract continue. We didn't do that. And that helped us during this year, but it was also a credit to the work that we had done on this collaboration leading up to COVID-19.

A middle school principal in a different district recounted a process different in details but similar in the rapid involvement of the key stakeholders:

> The onset of the pandemic led to a long list of new decisions that needed to be made quickly: schedule, instructional strategies, academic expectations, how to implement the new safety protocols, the social, emotional well-being of staff and students, just to name a few.

However, I felt fortunate here in [this district] because we had structures as well as a working mindset already in place, which allowed us to work together efficiently and effectively. . . . Our School Leadership Team is a critical structure which [the union vice president and I] built together and for which we serve as co-chairs. There's a principal, an association vice president, a supervisor, association reps, and grade-level and department team leaders. They make up the foundation, but there's always room for more, especially in a year like this. We felt the need to include our school nurse, a really important player on our SLT this year.

So while other districts were looking to assemble their mandated school-based restart and recovery teams, ours was ready to go. Sometimes, due to the nature of some of the decisions or the logistics of the situation, not every decision can be shared. But the goal of a collaborative organization is to share as many decisions as possible and be transparent when you can't.

The principal's union counterpart offered a very specific example of the work of the School Leadership Team in this crisis:

Our building, like most, has been operating on a hybrid schedule and dismissing before lunch so that all afternoon instruction happens virtually. We're preparing to move to a full day and serve lunch, which is not easy. So earlier this week, we had a School Leadership Team meeting and the administration came with a draft of a schedule that they had put together. And members of the School Leadership Team—teachers, guidance counselors, a nurse, paraprofessionals—had come with their own version of a draft. And we sat in a room, probably ten or twelve of us, hashing it out, talking about it. And seventy-five minutes later, we ended in a very different place from where we had begun.

Then, each of the members of the Solutions Team went out with the draft that we had agreed upon and solicited input. They held a series of six one-hour meetings, covering all the people in the building. Information and excellent ideas came from all different people. And once again, we were in a different place from where we started and are very close to a final decision.

Using collaborative structures takes more time than the top-down approach, but yields more workable, user-friendly results. Encouraging voice means more input, engagement, and passion and a sense of team, all of which makes our students' experiences richer.

She ended with this tribute to the process:

> Our SLT has worked to develop solutions related to the hybrid schedule, curriculum planning, and instructional needs. By working together collaboratively and hearing the needs of all involved, including staff, students, and the community, we've been able to tackle unprecedented challenges and situations that would otherwise have been nearly impossible.

Diversity, Equity, and Inclusion

Another recent challenge across multiple districts has been the increasing emphasis on Diversity, Equity, and Inclusion (DEI). A principal and union building representative from one of the early collaborative schools told their story:

> **PRINCIPAL:**
> There wasn't a lot of momentum at the district level with Professional Development to help staff grow in areas of DEI. The [School Leadership Team] formed a building-based DEI team that did a needs assessment and took initiative within the building. It provided six different Professional Development sessions, focused on different aspects of diversity and inclusion.
>
> **UNION BUILDING REPRESENTATIVE:**
> The content of DEI came on us like an avalanche. It was so big in so many ways. Some districts just dabbled in it. It's such a complex topic that most of us didn't understand. We didn't know where to focus. It was really messy.

We had outside consultants at the start who were effective. But the staff really appreciated learning from and with other staff members. The sessions and work were very meaningful because they were peer led—administrators and teachers sitting together and learning together, instead of listening to someone from outside.

Working effectively took us several years. It took the commitment of a lot of people over a lot of time. We're still moving toward it. We're definitely better at it than a couple of years ago. But you can't solve everything at once, you take pieces. The job of the DLT and SLT is to break things into manageable pieces.

LEADING-EDGE ISSUES FOR THE COLLABORATIVE

Involving More Stakeholders

The districts of the Collaborative, as we have indicated, have gradually widened the scope of included stakeholders. Local school boards have become active participants in several of our cases, and students have sometimes been brought in. These efforts, however, are still new, and we don't have a full structure or protocol for them.

Local school boards represent the voice of communities and parents in school governance. Though they vary in structure and composition across the country, in most cases—including New Jersey—they hire the superintendent but are supposed to stay out of direct involvement in school operations. They are supposed to see that the district is well managed but not manage the district themselves. This has created a dilemma for the Collaborative: clearly the local school boards are critical stakeholders in the system, but they are not supposed to be involved in the kind of discussions that concern the Leadership Teams at the district and school levels.

Nevertheless, a number of districts have found ways to push the boundaries. Two school board members from different districts have joined the peer Facilitation Team, working with a range of schools outside their own district. Several schools have set up regular channels of communication between collaborative teams and the local board, helping to build understanding and alignment without formal decision-making consensus. This has included having different School Leadership Teams take turns sharing their current activities at each public school board meeting.

But a good deal remains to be done to further clarify this relationship. It is still not clear, for instance, whether it is a good idea for school board members to serve on District Leadership Teams or whether other structures lead to more constructive discussion. As these relationships develop, the New Jersey School Boards Association is developing new orientation and training of new board members, and state regulators may need to revise some existing rules.

Similar issues arise with other stakeholders. Students have rarely been directly involved in committees of the Collaborative's schools. Should they be regular members of School Leadership Teams? Should they be invited onto improvement initiative teams that concern them, or should they serve only in consultative roles? How should the representatives be selected? The same questions apply to involvement by parents or the wider community.

We expect that these questions will be worked out in the usual method of the Collaborative: through experimentation in various districts, followed by discussion in interdistrict and role-alike sessions, to be then taken up by the State Support Group or the Facilitation Team (depending on the issue) to organize the learnings and codify them, bringing in any relevant parties.

A final important stakeholder is government, including the state and national departments of education. Their policies, of course, have enormous impact on schools, but there is (as of this writing) no mechanism for their involvement in the work of the Collaborative. In the early days of the Collaborative, neither side was interested in starting a conversation. The State Support Group deliberately avoided interference from an unsympathetic state governor. In the long run, however, the development of an interactive, collaborative educational system—after decades of policies pushing top-down, testing-focused regulation—cannot succeed without the support of governmental bodies. This will be an issue going forward.

This ongoing momentum to broaden the Collaborative to include more stakeholders has led to developments at the level of the State Support Group. The original leaders on the team from the various education-focused associations represent key stakeholders, but we also feel a need to engage others such as parent groups, students, and government. Moreover, the collaborative effort is only a small part of the jobs of the State Support Group: at this stage they each have members, especially among the peer facilitators, who have a far deeper involvement in the process. For the next phase, we are building a larger advisory board that includes many of the facilitators and other institutional representatives, who can engage directly with one another and their state organizations to advance the process.

Large, Urban, High-Poverty Districts

Like most states, New Jersey has a large gap between wealthy and high-poverty districts—particularly between suburbs and big urban centers, often with large minority populations. The Collaborative includes a healthy mix of this range: on a ranking of New Jersey districts by wealth, the participating districts range from near the top to the absolute bottom—and they average well below the midpoint.[1] Five of the twenty-five are high-poverty urban districts. But those five relatively recent additions joined not long before the COVID-19 crisis, so we have not yet gotten a full sense of what adjustments might be needed in the basic model.

The record so far is good: at least four of the five large urbans that have started the process are still active after several years, with functioning Leadership Teams at the district and school levels. (The fifth had a change of superintendent during the COVID years and the status is uncertain as of this writing). Three of those four are clearly moving forward with improvement initiatives; the fourth is actively struggling with long-standing divisions within the board and the administration, using the Collaborative's peer facilitators as a resource.

Leaders of two large urban districts describe their progress:

UNION LEADER:

When this concept was introduced to us, I didn't have that kumbaya moment: I literally sat there and rolled my eyes for 90 percent of the meeting because I never thought that that could work here. But going to the conferences, seeing how well it worked in other districts, I realized that we can do this here.

When the pandemic hit, it was the superintendent's team that reached out to us first because we were still in the process of gaining trust. He said, "You know, we're about to go through this pandemic, I want you to join our leadership team." And what happened was that our members started to have their voices heard.

SUPERINTENDENT:

[When the COVID pandemic hit], not only did [the union leader] sit on the executive team, there were twenty representatives on all of our sub-committees. It was not about contractual problems—it was really about instructional problems and how we can make teaching and learning better for our students. But the union team never really just came with the problems. They always came with additional solutions to the problem.

Large urban districts often have a high rate of turnover, particularly among superintendents. There are strong financial incentives, as well as reasons of work quality, for good leaders and staff to move out. The irony is that it is clear from the evidence shown in chapter 2, and from our experience, that effective collaboration substantially reduces turnover over time—but the initially high turnover rate is an obstacle to getting started.

We know that this vicious circle can be overcome: one of our models described in chapter 5, ABC Unified School District, is a high-poverty district that over a decade or so built enough trust that the situation stabilized, and new hires at all levels were committed to collaboration. In New Jersey, we are still fairly early in that process. At an interdistrict meeting, a superintendent from one of these districts said,

> My whole team is new, my whole cabinet team is new. And it was very important for me to invite my entire team here today so we can continue this sense of sustainability. Whether I'm here or anyone leaves, if we don't continue this work, then all the work that we have done in the past is for naught. So it's very important that as we discuss this as a group, that we also think about us as moving pieces.

We expect that there will be considerable future learning about the specific needs of large urban districts, learnings that will be incorporated in the Collaborative by the usual mechanisms of experimentation, sharing, and codification.

THE DEVELOPMENT OF TRUST

Finally, we want to touch on a central dynamic in all of these experiences: the development of trust. It is hard to pin down: like air, trust is essential to the life of collaboration but invisible and intangible. It can't be created through training or grand statements of intent; it needs to be built over time through experience. Participants need to see their partners in action, under stress, to test the depth of their humanity, honesty, and competence.

Bureaucracy is a system that seeks to eliminate the need for trust. Frederick Taylor developed his system of Scientific Management, with detailed mandates and close supervision, because he profoundly distrusted workers. That is a key reason bureaucracy is bad at innovation: innovation is always a risk, and so it requires the willingness to take risks with others.

Collaboration, on the other hand, requires a great deal of trust. In the pursuit of improvement, people have to move outside their defined roles, try new ideas, experiment; they must depend constantly on the goodwill of others and make themselves vulnerable to malicious actors. This is one major reason collaboration is hard, but it is also the reason it is much more resilient and innovative than bureaucracy.

The interactive processes we have described can be seen as a series of opportunities to demonstrate those qualities in action. In traditional union-management relations, all gambles are large ones: the parties meet primarily to settle contracts every three years or so. But in Collaborative Partnerships, when leaders meet frequently to discuss everyday problems, they can take low-risk gambles—propose untried approaches, make small concessions—and then they can see whether the other parties respond constructively and keep their word. And these tests can be repeated many times, each time adding to the store of trust, until participants become convinced that their counterparts are trustworthy. Teachers who have given up on participation because they have felt burned before by promises from their leaders can try it one more time, in a low-stakes way, and see whether it actually produces results. These participants can also get to know one another in new, more personal ways that remove them from their familiar roles—in informal meetings, over meals, in learning activities. They can see the people behind the roles, their motivations, what they truly care about.

In effect, all the interactive elements we have described—the workshops, the peer networks and facilitators, the partnership support teams and leadership teams—are deliberate trust-building mechanisms. Relationships develop through the constant interactions and outcomes of the partnership and the "web of support" that give people a chance to relax their defenses and to learn to work together. All the experiences we have sketched in this chapter—the overcoming of obstacles, the development of new structures and initiatives, the confronting of crises—have contributed to the store of trust.

A superintendent tells a story of his first steps in this trust-building process:

> I came to this with some armor on. And I was really guarded in my first couple of meetings. Then after my first couple of meetings, I realized that

there was something different. The conversation wasn't specifically about contractual issues—or rather, it was about contractual issues in terms of how best we can serve our students. And when your initial conversation is about teaching and learning, it really made me drop my guard and realize that this is what the real conversation should be about.

The union and the teachers said to me, "There are some gaps in your English language arts curriculum and in your pacing." But my team said, "No, there are not." So I said to the union, "Why don't you bring in your top teachers and let's get in a room with this and prove it to me." And they did!

I realized that this was totally different in terms of conversations. And that's when we first had a mutual respect that we were going to put students first and teachers first. And our decisions are going to be focused on what's best for students, regardless of our differences.

Through steps like these, the system gradually moves from a classic model, in which each person fills just one role and defends it against others, to one in which people can help one another and see the benefits of mutual exchange. It is this trust that breathes life and energy into collaboration, enabling people to take risks and to try untested improvements.[2]

CONCLUSION

These histories bring out some of the core strengths of the interactive approach to change. First, the process depends primarily on internal champions; external third parties are catalysts rather than drivers. Second, it systematically develops networks at every opportunity: networks within schools and districts, of course, but also, and even more important, networks across districts and institutions. Multiple districts come together twice a year for learning conferences, where they share stories like the ones sketched in this chapter. At those sessions and others, "role-alike" networks of principals, board members, union leaders, and superintendents share their experiences. Peer facilitators bring their leadership, knowledge, and experience to other districts as needed.

These networks provide durable webs of support. Principals who are having problems with their unions can reach out for help to other principals they have met through the role-alike network, to other union leaders through the facilitation network, or to the union representatives on the State Support Group. Board members doubtful about the effectiveness of the process can reach out to the state School Boards Association as well as to board members in other districts. Project teams running into blockages can hear from peers who have been through similar struggles.

The result is a cumulative learning process. Each district takes its own path, based on its own needs, context, and internal dynamics; but it also learns from the experiences of others so as to minimize dead ends and accelerate innovations. This "web of support" has also made the efforts unusually robust.

Thus there are, as we have seen in this chapter, many paths to success. Districts take on varied problems, and the champions come from varied parts of the system: in some cases, teachers take the lead; in others, union leaders; in others, superintendents or principals and, on occasion, school boards. These champions may feel frustrated and anxious at times, but the resources they find through the "web of support" help to sustain them, to develop new ideas, and to overcome resistance from other stakeholders.

A Superintendent looks back:

If you had asked me prior to our [entry] into the Collaborative, "'Is your district collaborative?,'" I would have said, probably like most, "Oh, of course, we collaborate," and I would have pointed my open door policy and the fact that everybody seems to be happy or satisfied, and that we solve problems. But it wasn't until we started our participation with the Collaborative, and those first couple of training sessions, that I realized we were really only on the surface collaborative. We didn't have structures and processes in place. And I thought maybe we were consulting, but maybe I wasn't really, maybe I was just asking questions of the people who would give me the answers I wanted to hear. And it was a very initially uncomfortable process for our district. But in going through that process, it really formalized this idea of working together on mutually agreed-upon areas to improve student learning and culture and climate.

There is still a long road ahead, and we foresee many obstacles in scaling to an entire state—to say nothing of an entire nation. The interactive approach is not a quick cure, but we believe it has already shown sufficient resilience and adaptiveness to offer a realistic alternative to the neoliberal approach of the past half century.

CHAPTER 10

Conclusion

W E BEGAN THIS BOOK with a criticism of the neoliberal paradigm that has been the dominant education policy framework of the past forty years. That approach, supported by both Democratic and Republican regimes, encourages decentralized market-driven educational initiatives such as charter schools and vouchers, while imposing centrally determined standards and rigorous testing across the system. The neoliberal approach has failed to improve the record of student performance that led to heavy criticism of public schooling since the 1970s. Indeed, student achievement has stagnated, teacher commitment has sharply declined, and a new mood of crisis has enveloped educational policy makers.

The efforts described in this book give reason for hope. We need now to return to two key questions: Do Collaborative Partnerships work better than the neoliberal paradigm? And can we get there from here?

THE EFFECTIVENESS OF COLLABORATIVE PARTNERSHIP

We have shown evidence in chapters 2 and 3 that Collaborative Partnership is associated with improved student performance in general and with reduced teacher turnover and greater teacher engagement, especially in high-poverty districts. There is a clear logic behind this improvement. If the major stakeholders of the system are aligned around a basic vision of improving teaching and learning, they are likely to achieve more than they would if they were fragmented, disillusioned, mistrustful, or confused.

The neoliberal approach destroys alignment. On one hand, it encourages fragmentation by encouraging parents to set up their own schools with their own priorities. On the other hand, it imposes a set of standards determined by experts and enforced by government through frequent and onerous testing that triggers financial and other sanctions. Teachers, who do the actual work, are not involved in either of these and are battered from both directions: they have to spend enormous amounts of class time preparing for tests and meeting mandates in which they have no say and much of the rest of their time managing parents who feel entitled to press for their often-conflicting agendas and demands. Administrators are often in conflict with their teachers as they try to hold the system together.

An effective collaborative system, by contrast, builds alignment by bringing stakeholders together in work focused on improving performance. This can produce important innovations and also improve relationships and trust throughout the system. We have seen details of these improvements in our descriptions of the New Jersey effort as well as others around the country: effective collaborative decision-making on the COVID-19 response; Diversity, Equity, and Inclusion initiatives; new curricula; introduction of technology; improving instructional practice; and other key issues. We have seen testimony from teachers, union leaders, administrators, board members, and other education leaders of their increased ability to work together.

It's not magic: not all schools that call themselves "collaborative" make such gains. Collaborative Partnership is a systemic change that takes time, effort, and goodwill, and there are many failures resulting from pseudo-collaboration or poor implementation. But in studies of hundreds of schools, we can see broad improvement—which is more than can be said for the neoliberal programs of recent decades.

We have built on a long experience of collaborative experiments in education as well as other industries. There have been many successes, but most have been isolated and temporary, fighting the strong neoliberal current.

We have added two important elements that seem to add robustness and resilience:

1. *Multi-stakeholder partnerships.* Most stakeholder partnerships in the past have been between unions and management. The New Jersey Collaborative has brought together other key parties in the educational venture—especially the school boards, as well as the state institutions representing superintendents and principals. There are still others who should be involved. But the point is that a multiparty dynamic is different from a dynamic involving just two parties: a multi-stakeholder partnership makes it more difficult for one stakeholder to disrupt the system from inside, and it engages forces that might disrupt the system from outside. The parties are interdependent in many ways and need one another's support. Thus, we have found that at the inevitable moments of tension and conflict in any organizational change, there are more points of leverage for moving forward.

2. *Webs of support.* Rather than relying on peak organizations such as government, nonprofits, or national organizations, the New Jersey Collaborative has built a network of relationships from the ground up. The mechanisms include regular meetings of the participating districts to learn from one another; "role-alike" networks of people with similar functions in different districts; and a network of facilitators drawn from experienced participants—teachers, superintendents, school board members, union representatives, principals—who can advise and support one another. When districts run into trouble—again, inevitably—they now regularly turn to these peer mechanisms for help.

GETTING THERE

Collaborative Partnership, as we have emphasized, is a system. It is not just a matter of good feelings and trusting relationships, though those are part of the picture. Collaborative Partnership also involves new structures and processes from the classroom through administration, unions, school boards, and governmental agencies. It cannot be established by fiat but requires substantial learning and changes in attitudes and habits at all these levels. Given those complexities, the fact that some districts, including the New Jersey Collaborative network we have focused on, have been able to make a good deal of progress is heartening.

We have shown that there is a plausible path to reliably scaling Collaborative Partnerships—one that draws on and develops the relations of trust in peer networks and that does not require sustained increases in spending (see chapter 8). But it is clear that this will be a long road, and there are substantial hurdles ahead.

At the district level, the New Jersey partner districts have generally made some immediate improvements, but changing the system as a whole takes time. Even our most advanced districts, which have been working actively in the Collaborative for more than nine years, are still finding enormous untapped potential and lingering conflicts. In chapter 9, we mentioned an advanced middle school that is directly involving half of its teachers in improvement task forces—an extraordinary achievement, but one that still leaves half of the teachers outside the circle. It will take more work to develop mechanisms through which *everyone* feels some involvement. This same school is proud of its success in engaging people in Diversity, Equity, and Inclusion processes, but at the same time the leaders feel there is a long way to go. At a system level, it would certainly take a decade, at the very least, to build a movement that could impact performance at the national level.

Moreover, there are many remaining hurdles, especially at the national level. Despite widespread bipartisan criticism of the current system—coming to something of a head in the last years of the Obama administration—the neoliberal approach is deeply embedded at levels with which we have just begun to engage, especially among many state and national policy makers and educational leaders.[1]

Government

As described in chapter 7, the New Jersey effort began in a hostile political environment; as a result, the state government has never been represented on the leadership team. Governor Phil Murphy personally endorsed the effort at a conference at Rutgers University in 2018, but there have been no sustained discussions about bringing the state Department of Education into the collaborative.

There were advantages to this way of starting the New Jersey Collaborative. Government involvement can stifle collaborative efforts because it puts the focus too far away from the classroom, where actual teaching and learning happen. When government is the primary sponsor, efforts tend to focus on large conferences, publications with broad distribution, and perhaps—if there is enough money—hiring consultants for training sessions. The financing is also unstable, dependent on the political winds. In the previous section we argued that our approach, which engages multiple stakeholders and builds a foundation primarily on webs of support from teachers and administrators in the schools, is a more resilient and robust form of intervention.

But clearly the active involvement of government will be essential over time. Government regulations and mandates are a constant concern and frequent irritant in the lives of teachers and administrators. We have often seen situations in which the regulators, if they only had a chance to see and talk with teachers in the classroom, might well change their views. So far, however, government representatives have remained almost entirely an external force, disengaged from the collaborative discussions.

We are increasingly of the view that government representatives should be part of the support team—but not dominant and not the main source of funding. It is crucial that the focus be on the educators and the parents, who are closest to the process of teaching and learning. Government agencies should understand those perspectives and take them into account, far more than at present, in formulating their mandates and standards.

National Associations and Unions

State-level association leaders have been involved from the origins of the New Jersey Collaborative's support team; these have included the associations of school boards, principals and supervisors, superintendents, and the state unions. As the Collaborative has grown, there has been increasing interest from leaders at the national level. But national institutions have not been continuously involved in the New Jersey Collaborative's discussions, and their activities often have the same generalized quality as government-sponsored programs: publishing news items, putting together informational binders, and producing other top-down initiatives. Because they are positioned at the top, they can have trouble grasping the importance of the "webs of support"—the peer networks of experience sharing and facilitation that create a resilient learning process across formal structural boundaries. Another layer of collaborative mechanisms is needed to engage these stakeholders—to keep them informed of progress and bring them directly into collaborative classrooms and peer learning networks so they can see the importance of this model of change.

Parents

Parents raise a somewhat different issue. They are obviously key stakeholders in the education system. They are formally represented by school boards, which are institutional partners in the Collaborative at the state and district levels. But currently, demands for more direct parental involvement are growing across the nation, driven especially by deep cultural differences concerning religion, gender, and race. Many communities are being torn apart by battles among parent groups, often demanding direct input into classroom curricula and methods.

The crisis is just starting to brew in New Jersey, but it seems that the demands for parental involvement are deeply rooted and will not disappear quickly. School boards will have to play a central role, since they are the democratically elected representatives of the parents. But to handle the tensions, local school boards may need to be more deeply engaged in the Collaborative than has been the case so far. The ABC Unified School District in California has been a pioneer in this effort; parents are regularly invited to collaborative events at the schools for direct discussion with teachers and administrators, which has helped to maintain community support in difficult periods of budget cuts and curriculum debates.

COLLABORATIVE PUBLIC EDUCATION AND DEMOCRACY

Many of the founding thinkers of the United States saw a close connection between a public system of education and the strength of a democratic system of government. Thomas Jefferson proposed a taxpayer-funded system of public education in 1779. Abraham Lincoln called it "the most important subject which we as a people can be engaged in."[2] Horace Mann, the driver of the development of the public education system in the nineteenth century, said it most emphatically: "Public education is the cornerstone of our community and our democracy."

These and other leaders saw public education as essential for creating a shared base of knowledge and tools for citizens discussing public policy and a common core of values and principles for the people as a whole. George Washington focused on this in his farewell address of 1796:

> The assimilation of the principles, opinions, and manners of our countrymen by the common education of a portion of our youth from every quarter well deserves attention. The more homogeneous our citizens can be made in these particulars the greater will be our prospect of permanent union; and a primary object of such a national institution should be the education of our youth in the science of government. In a republic what species of knowledge can be equally important and what duty more pressing on its legislature than to patronize a plan for communicating it to those who are to be the future guardians of the liberties of the country?[3]

A long line of social science literature has validated this view by demon-strating the empirical relation between effective public education and the strength of democracies.[4]

Washington's view, it is important to note, is a very *public* view of educa-tion. It is not compatible with a policy of radical choice: it sees the need for at least a shared "homogeneous" core of knowledge about government, and of "principles, opinions, and manners." John Adams extended the point:

> Reformation must begin with the body of the people, which can be done only, to effect, in their educations. The whole people must take upon them-selves the education of the whole people, and must be willing to bear the expenses of it. There should not be a district of one mile square, without a school in it, not founded by a charitable individual, but maintained at the expense of the people themselves.[5]

It is therefore particularly important that education be a part of demo-cratic discussion and decision-making. In a very general sense, of course, it already is: governance is controlled by elected political officials at state and national levels. But as indicated by the increasing political attacks on the system, the loss of confidence in public schools, and the increase in top-down control, those current democratic mechanisms are not adequate. They are not *working*; they are not achieving the broad public support neces-sary to the "permanent union" sought by Washington.[6]

In the current system, there is a very long path, with poor visibility, between the views of parents and the actions of policy makers. The result is increasing demand for direct parental involvement in their children's education, which has focused both the long-running movement for charter schools and vouchers and the more recent movement for transparency in curriculum. But teachers, highly educated and with strong professional identity, do not accept being dictated to about how they manage their class-rooms. The conflicts among visions of education have stoked feelings of anger and mistrust among all the parties, and the heavy-handed role of governments in imposing onerous mandates and standards from afar has added further fuel to the fire.

This suggests that education, which touches core values of the citizenry deeply and continuously, requires something more than occasional voting, the sporadic mechanism of democracy with which we are familiar. Education requires ongoing forums of discussion and problem-solving involving the multiple stakeholders—including parents, teachers, and administrators, as well as their representatives in unions, school boards, and governments. It requires, in fact, Collaborative Partnership.

This would be no more than an idealistic, utopian vision if it had not been shown to *work*—in districts across the country and in the New Jersey Collaborative network. These have shown that it is possible for schools to build trust among the disparate parties, to align around the value of improving teaching and learning, and to solve problems together. It is possible to build a system that sustains such relationships over time, rather than depending on the goodwill of transient individuals. It is possible to spread this system through networks of peer support and sharing. It is possible to achieve a form of democracy in which stakeholders engage actively with one another, rather than passing off disputes to distant representatives in political parties and government agencies.

We don't claim that the cases we have sketched in this book are complete ideals of Collaborative Partnership—we have noted a number of ways in which they need to be extended and improved. But they have indeed started on a path toward engaging the major parties in a shared effort to improve teaching and learning. Collaborative Partnership has demonstrated an ability to build trust among antagonistic parties and to build alignment among different contributors to the shared enterprise of education.

So we call on the leaders of national institutions—of governmental bodies, of unions, of school boards, of administrators, and of other stakeholder groups—to listen to their own agents in schools and districts around the country and to foster the development of the kind of collaborative mechanisms and networks we have described in this book. That would require a shift in the mentality of both the left and the right of the political spectrum: less focus on regulation and standards and also less emphasis on market competition. It would involve trusting the actors who are closest to the problem—the teachers, administrators, and parents, and their representatives in school boards and local unions—to develop improvements in teaching and learning. It encourages those national leaders to spend more time engaging with those on the front lines and finding ways to support their work.

Notes

CHAPTER 1

1. Frederick W. Taylor, *The Principles of Scientific Management* (New York: Harper Brothers, 1911); J. S. Brooks and M. T. Miles, "From Scientific Management to Social Justice . . . and Back Again? Pedagogical Shifts in Educational Leadership," *International Electronic Journal for Leadership in Learning*, January 2006; Raymond E. Callahan, *Education and the Cult of Efficiency* (University of Chicago Press, 1964); Kathy Emery, "Corporate Control of Public School Goals: High-Stakes Testing in Its Historical Perspective," *Teacher Education Quarterly* 34, no. 2 (2007): 25–44; Richard Nelson and Joseph Watras, "The Scientific Movement: American Education and the Emergence of the Technological Society," *Journal of Thought* 16, no. 1 (1981): 49–71.
2. Barbara Rogoff, Eugene Matusov, and Cynthia White, "Models of Teaching and Learning," in *The Handbook of Education and Human Development*, ed. David R. Olson and Nancy Torrance (Oxford: Blackwell Publishing, 2018), 373–98.
3. Callahan, *Education and the Cult of Efficiency*; Emery, "Corporate Control of Public School Goals"; Nelson and Watras, "Scientific Movement."
4. Diane Ravitch, *Left Back: A Century of Battles Over School Reform* (New York: Simon & Schuster, 2001), 164.
5. Callahan, *Education and the Cult of Efficiency*; Jeannie Oakes, "Tracking, Inequality, and the Rhetoric of Reform: Why Schools Don't Change," *Journal of Education* 168, no. 1 (January 1, 1986): 60–80.
6. Oakes, "Tracking, Inequality, and the Rhetoric of Reform."
7. Richard DuFour and Robert Eaker, *Professional Learning Communities at Work: Best Practices for Enhancing Student Achievement* (Bloomington, IN: National Educational Service. Solution Tree Press, 1998); Richard Dufour, Robert Eaker, and Rebecca Dufour, *Revisiting Professional Learning Communities at Work:*

New Insights for Improving Schools (Bloomington, IN: National Educational Service. Solution Tree Press, 2008).

8. L. Darling-Hammond and K. Montgomery, "Keeping the Promise: The Role of Policy in Reform," in *Keeping the Promise? The Debate over Charter Schools*, ed. L. Dingerson, B. Miner, B. Peterson, and S. Waters (Milwaukee: Rethinking Schools, 2008), 91–110.

9. Dick M. Carpenter and Scott L. Noller, "Measuring Charter School Efficiency: An Early Appraisal," *Journal of Education Finance* 35, no. 4 (2010): 397–415.

10. Milton Goldberg and James Harvey, "A Nation at Risk: The Report of the National Commission on Excellence in Education," *Phi Delta Kappan* 65, no. 1 (1983): 14–18.

11. Diane Ravitch, *Slaying Goliath: The Passionate Resistance to Privatization and the Fight to Save America's Public Schools* (New York: Knopf Doubleday Publishing Group, 2020).

12. Ravitch, *Slaying Goliath*; Jesse H. Rhodes, *An Education in Politics: The Origin and Evolution of No Child Left Behind* (Ithaca, NY: Cornell University Press, 2012).

13. Center for Research on Education Outcomes, "National Charter School Study," Stanford University, August 29, 2013, https://credo.stanford.edu/reports/item/national-charter-school-study/; Center for Research on Education Outcomes, "Online Charter School Study," Stanford University, August 31, 2015, https://credo.stanford.edu/reports/item/online-charter-school-study/.

14. Ravitch, *Slaying Goliath*.

15. Lisa Dragoset et al., "Race to the Top: Implementation and Relationship to Student Outcomes," NCEE 2017–4001, US Department of Education, Institute of Education Sciences, and National Center for Education Evaluation and Regional Assistance, October 2016, http://files.eric.ed.gov/fulltext/ED569959.pdf.

16. RAND Corporation, *Improving Teaching Effectiveness—Final Report: The Intensive Partnerships for Effective Teaching Through 2015–2016* (Santa Monica, CA: RAND Corporation, 2018), https://bit.ly/3qLsa2h.

17. Michelle Hackman and Eric Morath, "Teachers Quit Jobs at Highest Rate on Record," *Wall Street Journal*, December 28, 2018; Institute of Education Sciences, "Report on the Condition of Education 2021" (Washington, DC: US Department of Education, 2021).

18. This perspective is not new—it has a long history in industrial relations under the name of *institutionalism* or *pluralism*. See H. A. Clegg, "Pluralism in Industrial Relations," *British Journal of Industrial Relations* 13, no. 3 (November 1975): 309–16; John W. Budd and Stefan Zagelmeyer, "Public Policy and Employee Participation," in *The Oxford Handbook of Participation in Organizations*, ed. A. Wilkinson et al. (Oxford University Press, 2007), 476–503.

19. Clegg, "Pluralism in Industrial Relations"; Budd and Zagelmeyer, "Public Policy and Employee Participation."

CHAPTER 2

1. Michael Fullan, *Leading in a Culture of Change* (San Francisco: Jossey-Bass, 2001).
2. Robert Evans, *The Human Side of School Change: Reform, Resistance, and the Real-Life Problems of Innovation* (Hoboken, NJ: John Wiley & Sons, 2001).
3. Louise Stoll et al., "Professional Learning Communities: A Review of the Literature," *Journal of Educational Change* 7, no. 4 (November 28, 2006): 221–58.
4. Saul A. Rubinstein and John E. McCarthy, "Union–Management Partnerships, Teacher Collaboration, and Student Performance," *ILR Review* 69, no. 5 (July 21, 2016): 1114–32; Saul A. Rubinstein and John E. McCarthy, *Teachers Unions and Management Partnerships: How Working Together Improves Student Achievement* (Washington, DC: Center for American Progress, 2014).
5. These included the California Standards Tests, or CSTs; the California Alternate Performance Assessment, or CAPA; the California Modified Assessment; and, for high school students, the California High School Exit Examination, or CAHSEE.
6. The average API score for the district in 2011 was 834.
7. Rubinstein and McCarthy, "Union–Management Partnerships.
8. We had to remove three schools from our sample because their populations were outliers, or they did not administer standardized tests.
9. Psychological safety is the extent to which one perceives that one can be open and question policies or decisions without fear of reprisal.
10. Noe Medina and D. Monty Neill, *Fallout from the Testing Explosion: How 100 Million Standardized Exams Undermine Equity and Excellence in America's Public Schools*, 3rd rev. ed. (Cambridge, MA: National Center for Fair & Open Testing, March 1990), http://files.eric.ed.gov/fulltext/ED318749.pdf.
11. National Center for Education Statistics, "Table 204.10: Number and Percentage of Public School Students Eligible for Free or Reduced-Price Lunch, by State: Selected Years, 2000–01 Through 2015–16," *Digest of Education Statistics, 2017* (Washington, DC: Institute of Education Sciences), accessed December 9, 2022, https://nces.ed.gov/programs/digest/d17/tables/dt17_204.10.asp.
12. Geoffrey D. Borman et al., "Comprehensive School Reform and Achievement: A Meta-Analysis," *Review of Educational Research* 73, no. 2 (June 1, 2003): 125–230.
13. Yvonne L. Goddard, Roger D. Goddard, and Megan Tschannen-Moran, "A Theoretical and Empirical Investigation of Teacher Collaboration for School Improvement and Student Achievement in Public Elementary Schools," *Teachers College Record: The Voice of Scholarship in Education* 109, no. 4 (April 2007): 877–96, https://doi.org/10.1177/016146810710900401.

14. Frits K. Pil and Carrie Leana, "Applying Organizational Research to Public School Reform: The Effects of Teacher Human and Social Capital on Student Performance," *Academy of Management Journal* 52, no. 6 (2009): 1101–24.

15. Richard DuFour and Robert Eaker, *Professional Learning Communities at Work: Best Practices for Enhancing Student Achievement* (Bloomington, IN: National Educational Service. Solution Tree Press, 1998).

16. This research is summarized in Goddard, Goddard, and Tschannen-Moran, "A Theoretical and Empirical Investigation," 881.

17. Melissa Kay Diliberti and Heather L. Schwartz, *Districts Continue to Struggle with Staffing, Political Polarization, and Unfinished Instruction Selected Findings from the Fifth American School District Panel Survey* (RAND Corporation and American School District Panel, 2022), https://www.rand.org/content/dam/rand/pubs/research_reports/RRA900/RRA956-13/RAND_RRA956-13.pdf.

18. Mark Lieberman, "All Teaching Shortages Are Not Equal: 4 Takeaways From New Research," *Education Week*, December 6, 2022, https://www.edweek.org/leadership/all-teaching-shortages-are-not-equal-4-takeaways-from-new-research/2022/12.

19. Institute of Education Sciences, *Report on the Condition of Education 2021* (Washington, DC: US Department of Education, 2021); Lieberman, "All Teaching Shortages Are Not Equal."

20. G. H. Elder Jr., T. V. Nguyen, and A. Caspi, "Linking Family Hardship to Children's Lives," *Child Development* 56, no. 2 (April 1985): 361–75.

21. David Hursh, "Assessing No Child Left Behind and the Rise of Neoliberal Education Policies," *American Educational Research Journal* 44, no. 3 (September 1, 2007): 493–518.

22. Saul Rubinstein and John McCarthy, "The Future of U.S. Public School Reform: Elevating Teacher Voice," in *Revaluing Work(ers): Toward a Democratic and Sustainable Future*, ed. Tobias Schulze-Cleven and Todd E. Vachon, Labor and Employment Relations Association Series (Ithaca, NY: Labor and Employment Research Association, an imprint of Cornell University Press, 2021).

23. Rubinstein and McCarthy, "Future of U.S. Public School Reform."

24. John E. McCarthy and J. R. Keller, "How Managerial Openness to Voice Shapes Internal Attraction: Evidence from United States School Systems," *ILR Review* 75, no. 4 (August 1, 2022): 1001–23.

CHAPTER 3

1. Saul Rubinstein and John McCarthy, "The Future of U.S. Public School Reform: Elevating Teacher Voice," in *Revaluing Work(ers): Toward a Democratic and Sustainable Future*, ed. Tobias Schulze-Cleven and Todd E. Vachon, Labor and Employment Relations Series (Ithaca, NY: Labor and Employment Research Association, an imprint of Cornell University Press, 2021).

2. Charles Heckscher, *The New Unionism: Employee Involvement in the Changing Corporation*, 2nd ed. (New York: Basic Books, 1996; first published 1988); Thomas A. Kochan and Paul Osterman, *The Mutual Gains Enterprise: Forging a Winning Partnership Among Labor, Management, and Government* (Cambridge, MA: Harvard Business School Press, 1994); Ariel Avgar and Sarosh Kuruvilla, "Dual Alignment of Industrial Relations Activity: From Strategic Choice to Mutual Gains," in *Advances in Industrial and Labor Relations*, ed. Lewin David, E. Kaufman Bruce, and J. Gollan Paul, vol. 18 (Bingley, UK: Emerald Group Publishing Limited, 2011), 1–39; Todd E. Vachon and Josef Kuo-Hsun Ma, "Bargaining for Success: Examining the Relationship Between Teacher Unions and Student Achievement," *Sociological Forum* 30, no. 2 (June 2015): 391–414, https://doi.org/10.1111/socf.12168; Saul A. Rubinstein and Thomas A. Kochan, *Learning from Saturn: Possibilities for Corporate Governance and Employee Relations* (Ithaca, NY: ILR Press, 2001).

3. Caroline Minter Hoxby, "How Teachers' Unions Affect Education Production," *Quarterly Journal of Economics* 111, no. 3 (1996): 671–718; Terry M. Moe, "Collective Bargaining and the Performance of the Public Schools," *American Journal of Political Science* 53, no. 1 (January 2009): 156–74.

4. Exceptions include Susan Moore Johnson, *Teacher Unions in Schools* (Philadelphia, PA: Temple University Press, 1984); Charles Taylor Kerchner, Julia E. Koppich, and Joseph G. Weeres, *United Mind Workers: Unions and Teaching in the Knowledge Society*, Jossey-Bass Education Series (San Francisco: Jossey-Bass, 1997).

5. Frits K. Pil and Carrie Leana, "Applying Organizational Research to Public School Reform: The Effects of Teacher Human and Social Capital on Student Performance," *Academy of Management Journal* 52, no. 6 (2009): 1101–24; Ray Reagans and Ezra W. Zuckerman, "Networks, Diversity, and Productivity: The Social Capital of Corporate R&D Teams," *Organization Science* 12, no. 4 (August 1, 2001): 502–17.

6. For example, Moe, "Collective Bargaining and the Performance of the Public Schools."

7. Saul A. Rubinstein and John E. McCarthy, *Teachers Unions and Management Partnerships: How Working Together Improves Student Achievement* (Washington, DC: Center for American Progress, 2014).

8. Rubinstein and McCarthy, *Teachers Unions and Management Partnerships*.

9. John E. McCarthy, "Catching Fire: Institutional Interdependencies in Union-Facilitated Knowledge Diffusion," *British Journal of Industrial Relations* 57, no. 1 (March 2019): 182–201.

10. Henry William Chesbrough, *Open Innovation: The New Imperative for Creating and Profiting from Technology* (Cambridge, MA: Harvard Business Press, 2003).

11. Deborah Gladstein Ancona, "Outward Bound: Strategic for Team Survival in an Organization," *Academy of Management Journal* 33, no. 2 (June 1, 1990): 334–65; Morten T. Hansen, Joel M. Podolny, and Jeffrey Pfeffer, "So Many Ties, So Little Time: A Task Contingency Perspective on Corporate Social Capital in

Organizations," *Social Capital of Organizations,* 18 (June 11, 2001): 21–57, https://doi.org/10.1016/s0733-558x(01)18002-x.

12. Louise Stoll and Karen Seashore Louis, eds., *Professional Learning Communities: Divergence, Depth, and Dilemmas* (London: McGraw-Hill Education, 2007), 7.

13. A. Hargreaves and C. Giles, "The Knowledge Society School: An Endangered Entity," in *Teaching in the Knowledge Society,* ed. Andy Hargreaves (New York: Teachers College Press, 2003), 127–59.

14. Louise Stoll et al., "What Is a Professional Learning Community? A Summary," in *Creating and Sustaining Effective Professional Learning Communities* (DfES Research Report RR637, University of Bristol, 2005), http://www.louisestoll.com/wp-content/uploads/2020/07/PLC-source-materials_Summary-1.pdf; A. Hargreaves and C. Giles, "The Knowledge Society School: An Endangered Entity," in *Teaching in the Knowledge Society,* ed. Andy Hargreaves (New York: Teachers College Press, 2003), 127–59; Richard DuFour et al., *Revisiting Professional Learning Communities at Work: Proven Insights for Sustained, Substantive School Improvement* (Bloomington, IN: Solution Tree, 2021).

15. Michael Fullan, *All Systems Go: The Change Imperative for Whole System Reform* (Thousand Oaks, CA: Corwin Press, 2010).

16. McCarthy, "Catching Fire."

17. Vanessa Urch Druskat and Jane V. Wheeler, "Managing from the Boundary: The Effective Leadership of Self-Managing Work Teams," *Academy of Management Journal* 46, no. 4 (August 1, 2003): 435–57.

18. Ajay Mehra et al., "The Social Network Ties of Group Leaders: Implications for Group Performance and Leader Reputation," *Organization Science* 17, no. 1 (February 1, 2006): 64–79.

19. Jennifer A. Marrone, Paul E. Tesluk, and Jay B. Carson, "A Multilevel Investigation of Antecedents and Consequences of Team Member Boundary-Spanning Behavior," *Academy of Management Journal* 50, no. 6 (2007): 1423–39; Howard Aldrich and Diane Herker, "Boundary Spanning Roles and Organization Structure," *AMRO* 2, no. 2 (April 1, 1977): 217–30.

20. Mehra et al., "The Social Network Ties of Group Leaders."

21. McCarthy, "Catching Fire."

22. D. Z. Levin and R. Cross, "The Strength of Weak Ties You Can Trust: The Mediating Role of Trust in Effective Knowledge Transfer," *Management Science* 50, no. 11 (2004): 1477–90.

23. McCarthy, "Catching Fire"; John E. McCarthy, "Labor-Management Partnerships' Effects on Unionists' Interaction Networks: Evidence from U.S. Public Schools," *Industrial Relations* 60, no. 3 (July 2021): 277–306.

24. McCarthy, "Labor-Management Partnerships' Effects."

25. John E. McCarthy and J. R. Keller, "How Managerial Openness to Voice Shapes Internal Attraction: Evidence from United States School Systems," *ILR Review* 75, no. 4 (August 1, 2022): 1001–23.

26. Rubinstein and Kochan, *Learning from Saturn*; Saul A. Rubinstein, "The Impact of Co-management on Quality Performance: The Case of the Saturn Corporation," *Industrial & Labor Relations Review*, 2000, 197–218; Saul A. Rubinstein, "The Local Union Revisited: New Voices from the Front Lines," *Industrial Relations* 40, no. 3 (July 2001): 405; Bruce E. Kaufman and David I. Levine, "An Economic Analysis of Employee Representation," in *Nonunion Employee Representation: History, Contemporary Practice, and Policy*, ed. Bruce E. Kaufman and Daphne Gottlieb Taras (Armonk, NY: M.E. Sharpe, 2000), 149.

27. Avgar and Kuruvilla, "Dual Alignment of Industrial Relations Activity."

28. "New Jersey Public School Labor-Management Collaborative Gets National Attention," Patrick Rumaker, Editor, NJEA Review, New Jersey Education Association, October 5, 2021, https://www.njea.org/cardona-pringle-elevate-labor -management-collaboration-in-delran/.

29. "New Jersey Public School Labor-Management Collaborative Gets National Attention."

30. "New Jersey Public School Labor-Management Collaborative Gets National Attention."

CHAPTER 4

1. P. F. Drucker, *Concept of the Corporation* (New York: John Day, 1946); A. D. Chandler, *The Visible Hand: The Managerial Revolution in American Business* (Cambridge, MA: Harvard University Press, 1977).

2. W. G. Ouchi, *Theory Z: How American Business Can Meet the Japanese Challenge* (Reading, MA: Addison-Wesley, 1982); Richard T. Pascale and Anthony G. Athos, *The Art of Japanese Management: Applications for American Executives* (New York: Warner Books, 1981); J. P. Womack, D. Roos, and D. T. Jones, *The Machine That Changed the World* (New York: Macmillan, 1990).

3. Charles Heckscher, *The Collaborative Enterprise* (New Haven, CT: Yale University Press, 2007).

4. Heckscher, *Collaborative Enterprise*.

5. G. Hamel, "Waking up IBM: How a Gang of Unlikely Rebels Transformed Big Blue," *Harvard Business Review* 78, no. 4 (2000): 137–46.

6. Paul Adler, Charles Heckscher, and Laurence Prusak, "Building a Collaborative Enterprise," *Harvard Business Review* 89, no. 7–8 (2011): 94–101; Charles Heckscher and Paul S. Adler, eds., *The Firm as a Collaborative Community: Reconstructing Trust in the Knowledge Economy* (Oxford: Oxford University Press, 2006).

7. David Lewin et al., "Getting It Right: Empirical Evidence and Policy Implications from Research on Public-Sector Unionism and Collective Bargaining," *Employment Policy Research Network* Report 2011.

8. Masahiko Aoki, *Information, Incentives and Bargaining in the Japanese Economy: A Microtheory of the Japanese Economy* (Cambridge: Cambridge University Press, 1988); Masahiko Aoki, "Toward an Economic Model of the Japanese Firm," *Journal of Economic Literature* 28, no. 1 (1990): 1–27.

9. Heckscher, *Collaborative Enterprise*; David Levine and Laura D'Andrea Tyson, "Participation, Productivity, and the Firm's Environment," in *Paying for Productivity: A Look at Evidence*, ed. Alan S. Blinder (Washington, Brookings Institute, 1990).

10. Richard Barry Freeman and Joel Rogers, *What Workers Want* (Ithaca, NY: Cornell University Press, 2006).

11. Sumner H. Slichter, *Union Policies and Industrial Management* (Washington, DC: Brookings Institution, 1941).

12. Slichter, *Union Policies and Industrial Management*.

13. Neil Chamberlain et al., "The Impact of Collective Bargaining on Management," *Industrial & Labor Relations Review* 14, no. 4 (July 1961): 622; Clinton S. Golden, Harold J. Ruttenberg, and Frank C. Pierson, "The Dynamics of Industrial Democracy," *Science and Society* 6, no. 4 (1942): 383–85.

14. Saul A. Rubinstein, "The Local Union Revisited: New Voices from the Front Lines," *Industrial Relations* 40, no. 3 (July 2001): 405.

15. Heckscher, *Collaborative Enterprise*.

16. Saul A. Rubinstein and Thomas A. Kochan, *Learning from Saturn: Possibilities for Corporate Governance and Employee Relations* (Ithaca, NY: ILR Press, 2001).

17. Based on J.D. Power Consumer Verified Ratings from 1993 through 1998.

18. Saul Rubinstein, Michael Bennett, and Thomas Kochan, "The Saturn Partnership: Co-management and the Reinvention of the Local Union," in *Employee Representation: Alternatives and Future Directions*, ed. Bruce Kaufman and Morris Kleiner (Madison, WI: Industrial Relations Research Association, 1993), 339–70.

19. Saul A. Rubinstein, "The Impact of Co-management on Quality Performance: The Case of the Saturn Corporation," *Industrial & Labor Relations Review*, 2000, 197–218.

20. M. S. Granovetter, "The Strength of Weak Ties," *American Journal of Sociology* 78, no. 6 (1973): 1360–80; M. Granovetter, "Economic Action and Social Structure: The Problem of Embeddedness," *American Journal of Sociology* 91, no. 3 (1985): 481.

21. David Knoke and James H. Kuklinski, *Network Analysis* (Beverly Hills, CA: Sage, 1982).

22. David Krackhardt and Henry Mintzberg, "Power in and Around Organizations," *Administrative Science Quarterly* 30, no. 4 (December 1985): 597; Haruo Shimada and John Paul MacDuffie, "Industrial Relations and 'Humanware'" (Working paper no. 1855-87, Alfred P. Sloan School of Management, Massachusetts Institute of Technology, December 1986), https://dspace.mit.edu/bitstream

/handle/1721.1/48159/industrialrelatiooshim.pdf;sequence=1; Kiyoshi Suzaki, *New Manufacturing Challenge: Techniques for Continuous Improvement* (New York: Simon & Schuster, 1987); Robert H. Hayes et al., *Dynamic Manufacturing: Creating the Learning Organization* (New York: Simon & Schuster, 1988).

23. E. L. Trist, *The Evolution of Socio-Technical Systems* (Toronto: Ontario Quality of Working Life Centre, Ontario Ministry of Labour, 1981), https://www.lmmiller .com/blog/wp-content/uploads/2013/06/The-Evolution-of-Socio-Technical -Systems-Trist.pdf.

24. Joseph M. Juran, *Managerial Breakthrough: A New Concept of the Manager's Job* (New York: McGraw-Hill, 1964).

25. Saul A. Rubinstein et al., "The Saturn Partnership: Co-management and the Reinvention of the Local Union."

26. Heckscher, *Collaborative Enterprise.*

27. Robert M. Grant, "Strategic Planning in a Turbulent Environment: Evidence from the Oil Majors," *Strategic Management Journal* 24, no. 6 (June 2003): 491–517; Torben Juul Andersen, "Integrating Decentralized Strategy Making and Strategic Planning Processes in Dynamic Environments," *Journal of Management Studies* 41, no. 8 (2004): 1271–99; Charles Heckscher, "Shared Purpose," in *The Collaborative Enterprise* (New Haven, CT: Yale University Press, 2007); Richard Whittington, *Opening Strategy: Professional Strategists and Practice Change, 1960 to Today* (Oxford: Oxford University Press, 2019).

28. Charles Heckscher and Nathaniel Foote, "The Strategic Fitness Process and the Creation of Collaborative Communities," in *The Firm as a Collaborative Community: Reconstructing Trust in the Knowledge Economy,* ed. Charles Heckscher and Paul S. Adler (Oxford: Oxford University Press, 2006), 479–512.

29. Michael Beer, Russell A. Eisenstat, and Bert Spector, "Why Change Programs Don't Produce Change," *Harvard Business Review,* November–December 1990, 158–66.

CHAPTER 5

1. Richard DuFour, Rebecca Burnette DuFour, and Robert E. Eaker, *Revisiting Professional Learning Communities at Work: New Insights for Improving Schools* (Bloomington, IN: Solution Tree, 2008).

2. Julia Koppich, "Addressing Teacher Quality Through Induction, Professional Compensation, and Evaluation: The Effects on Labor-Management Relations," *Educational Policy* 19, no. 1 (January 1, 2005): 90–111.

3. Saul A. Rubinstein and John E. McCarthy, "Public School Reform Through Union-Management Collaboration," in *Advances in Industrial and Labor Relations,* ed. Lewin David and J. Gollan Paul, vol. 20 (Bingley, UK: Emerald Group Publishing, 2012), 1–50; Saul A. Rubinstein and John E. McCarthy, *Reforming Public*

School Systems through Sustained Union-Management Collaboration (Washington, DC: Center for American Progress, July 2011), http://files.eric.ed.gov/fulltext /ED536074.pdf.

4. We do not name districts other than the ABC Unified School District for reasons of confidentiality.

CHAPTER 6

1. Bill Roche and John Geary, *Partnership at Work: The Quest for Radical Organizational Change* (New York: Routledge, 2006); John Kelly, "Social Partnership Agreements in Britain: Labor Cooperation and Compliance," *Industrial Relations* 43, no. 1 (January 2004): 267–92.

2. William N. Cooke, *Labor-Management Cooperation: New Partnerships or Going in Circles?* (Kalamazoo, MI: W.E. Upjohn Institute for Employment Research, 1990); William N. Cooke, "Product Quality Improvement through Employee Participation: The Effects of Unionization and Joint Union-Management Administration," *ILR Review* 46, no. 1 (October 1, 1992): 119–34; J. Cutcher-Gershenfeld, R. B. McKersie, and R. E. Walton, "Dispute Resolution and the Transformation of U.S. Industrial Relations: A Negotiations Perspective" (Working paper no. 3056-89-BPS, Alfred P. Sloan School of Management, Massachusetts Institute of Technology, August 1989), https://dspace.mit.edu/bitstream/ handle/1721.1/47207/disputeresolutiooocutc.pdf%3Bjsessionid%3DCC0473E7 EF5864D92134ADE636C6FD8E?sequence%3D1 A. E. Eaton and P. B. V. Voos, *Unions and Contemporary Innovations in Work Organization, Compensation, and Employee Participation* (Kingston, Ontario: Queens University, Industrial Relations Centre, 1989), https://irc.queensu.ca/wp-content/uploads/articles/articles _QPIR-eaton-voos-unions-and-contemporary-inovations-in-work-organization -compensation-and-employee-participation.pdf.

3. Saul A. Rubinstein, "The Local Union Revisited: New Voices from the Front Lines," *Industrial Relations* 40, no. 3 (July 2001): 405.

4. John E. McCarthy, "Labor-Management Partnerships' Effects on Unionists' Interaction Networks: Evidence from U.S. Public Schools," *Industrial Relations* 60, no. 3 (July 2021): 300–301.|

5. Unpublished research by John McCarthy, described in chapter 3.

6. Saul Rubinstein and John McCarthy, "The Future of U.S. Public School Reform: Elevating Teacher Voice," in *Revaluing Work(ers): Toward a Democratic and Sustainable Future*, ed. Tobias Schulze-Cleven and Todd E. Vachon, Labor and Employment Relations Series (Ithaca, NY: Labor and Employment Research Association, an imprint of Cornell University Press, 2021).

7. McCarthy, "Labor-Management Partnerships' Effects."

8. McCarthy, "Labor-Management Partnerships' Effects."

9. Rubinstein, "Local Union Revisited," 418.

10. Rubinstein, "Local Union Revisited," 424.
11. "NEA, NJEA Strengthen Partnership to Grow Labor-Management Collaboration," *NJEA News*, March 24, 2021, https://www.njea.org/nea-njea-strengthen -partnership-to-grow-labor-management-collaboration/.
12. "NEA President and U.S Education Secretary Focus on Labor-Management Collaboration," Patrick Rumaker, Editor, *NJEA Review*, New Jersey Education Association, NEA Today, September 14, 2021. https://www.nea.org/advocating -for-change/new-from-nea/nea-president-and-us-education-secretary-focus-labor -management-collaboration.

CHAPTER 7

1. Geoffrey D. Borman et al., "Comprehensive School Reform and Achievement: A Meta-Analysis," *Review of Educational Research* 73, no. 2 (June 1, 2003): 125–230.
2. W. Patrick Dolan and Lilot Moorman, *Restructuring Our Schools: A Primer on Systemic Change* (Kansas City, MO: Systems & Organization, 1994).
3. "New Jersey Public School Labor-Management Collaborative Gets National Attention," Patrick Rumaker, Editor, NJEA Review, New Jersey Education Association, October 5, 2021, https://www.njea.org/cardona-pringle-elevate-labor -management-collaboration-in-delran/; "National Education Leaders See How Rutgers Research Supports K-12 Student Success," Steve Flamisch, Rutgers Today, Rutgers, The State University of New Jersey, September 9, 2021, https:// www.rutgers.edu/news/national-education-leaders-visit-nj-see-how-rutgers -research-supports-k-12-student-success.

CHAPTER 8

1. Frederick W. Taylor, *The Principles of Scientific Management* (New York: Harper Brothers, 1911).
2. Daan van Knippenberg and Sim B. Sitkin, "A Critical Assessment of Charismatic–Transformational Leadership Research: Back to the Drawing Board?," *Academy of Management Annals* 7, no. 1 (2013): 1–60.
3. Michael Beer, Russell A. Eisenstat, and Bert Spector, "Why Change Programs Don't Produce Change," *Harvard Business Review*, November–December 1990, 158–66.
4. Bradley J. Hastings and Gavin M. Schwarz, "Leading Change Processes for Success: A Dynamic Application of Diagnostic and Dialogic Organization Development," *Journal of Applied Behavioral Science* 58, no. 1 (March 1, 2022): 120–48. *The Critical Path to Corporate Renewal,* by Michael Beer, Russell A. Eisenstat, and Bert Spector (Cambridge, MA: Harvard Business Press, 1990), is one of the more clearly formulated examples of a mixed approach.

5. Laura Singleton, "Understanding the Evolution of Theoretical Constructs in Organization Studies: Examining 'Purpose,'" in *Academy of Management Annual Meeting Proceedings* 2014, no. 1 (October 2014): 14367; Elaine Hollensbe et al., "Organizations with Purpose," *Academy of Management Journal* 57, no. 5 (October 1, 2014): 1227–34; Ed Catmull, "Building a Sense of Purpose at Pixar," *McKinsey Quarterly*, April 2014, http://www.mckinsey.com/Insights/Media_Entertainment /Building_a_sense_of_purpose_at_Pixar?cid=other-eml-alt-mkq-mck-oth-1404.

6. We previously discussed the research on, and practice of, past partnerships in chapters 3 through 6.

7. Clive Colling and Lee Harvey, "Quality Control, Assurance and Assessment— the Link to Continuous Improvement," *Quality Assurance in Education*, 3, no. 4 (December 1995): 30–34, https://doi.org/10.1108/09684889510098168; Kiyoshi Suzaki, *New Manufacturing Challenge: Techniques for Continuous Improvement* (New York: Simon & Schuster, 1987); Souraj Salah, Juan A. Carretero, and Abdur Rahim, "The Integration of Quality Management and Continuous Improvement Methodologies with Management Systems," *International Journal of Productivity and Quality Management* 6, no. 3 (2010): 269–88, https://doi.org/10.1504/ijpqm .2010.035116; Joseph M. Juran, *Managerial Breakthrough: A New Concept of the Manager's Job* (New York: McGraw-Hill, 1964).

8. These structures draw on a long history of union-management partnerships and Quality-of-Work-Life efforts. We saw in chapter 5 that they were developed independently in some form in all our study districts. In naming them the District Leadership Team and the School Leadership Team, we drew in part from the work of Patrick Dolan and the Consortium for Educational Change.

9. The Fishbone tool, also called the Ishikawa Diagram, is widely available—for example at https://asq.org/quality-resources/fishbone. We have adapted this from available training materials. For the Solutions Matrix, also adapted from public materials, the participants construct a table with potential solutions on the vertical axis and key criteria for evaluating solutions on the horizontal axis—such as the likely effectiveness of the solution, the resources and time required, and other criteria as needed.

10. Desert Survival is a standard exercise widely available in various books and training packages. We have adapted it the school setting.

11. This was originally based on a seven-step continuum from the Consortium for Educational Change. We tried simplifying it to three categories, but some of our initial districts preferred five steps—and so it has remained.

12. Geoffrey D. Borman et al., "Comprehensive School Reform and Achievement: A Meta-Analysis," *Review of Educational Research* 73, no. 2 (June 1, 2003): 125–230.

13. Philip J. Maxton, "Embracing Both Diagnostic and Dialogic Forms of Organization Development in Order to Exploit and Explore," *Journal of Applied Behavioral Science* 57, no. 1 (March 1, 2021): 125–28; Hastings and Schwarz, "Leading Change Processes for Success."

14. Robert E. Slavin and Nancy A. Madden, "Roots & Wings: Effects of Whole-School Reform on Student Achievement," *Journal of Education for Students Placed at Risk* 5, no. 1–2 (April 2000): 109–36.
15. County Health Rankings & Roadmaps, "Comprehensive School Reform," University of Wisconsin Population Health Institute, June 21, 2018, https://www .countyhealthrankings.org/take-action-to-improve-health/what-works-for-health /strategies/comprehensive-school-reform.

CHAPTER 9

1. Based on data from a 2017 survey of NY districts: https://patch.com/new-jersey /parsippany/new-jerseys-wealthiest-poorest-school-districts-2017. At that time the districts of the Collaborative averaged in the 41st percentile. Since then most of our additional districts have been from high-poverty areas.
2. Charles Heckscher, *Trust in a Complex World: Rebuilding Community* (Oxford: Oxford University Press, 2015), chap. 6.

CHAPTER 10

1. Diane Ravitch, *The Death and Life of the Great American School System: How Testing and Choice Are Undermining Education* (New York: Basic Books, 2011); Paul E. Peterson, "Bush-Obama Regulations Fail to Generate Sustained Gains in Student Achievement" (press release, Harvard Kennedy School, May 10, 2016), https:// www.hks.harvard.edu/announcements/bush-obama-regulations-fail-generate -sustained-gains-student-achievement.
2. Abraham Lincoln, "First Campaign Statement (March 9, 1832)" (speech given to the people of Sangamo County, March 9, 1832), *Lincoln's Writings*, edited by Matthew Pinsker (Carlisle, PA: Dickinson College), https://housedivided.dickinson .edu/sites/lincoln/first-campaign-statement-march-9-1832.
3. George Washington, "Washington's Farewell Address" (speech, Washington, DC, 1796), *The Avalon Project: Documents in Law, History, and Diplomacy* (New Haven, CT: Lillian Goldman Law Library, Yale Law School), http://avalon.law.yale.edu /18th_century/washing.asp.
4. Seymour Martin Lipset, "Some Social Requisites of Democracy: Economic Development and Political Legitimacy1," *American Political Science Review* 53, no. 1 (March 1959): 69–105; Edward L. Glaeser, Giacomo A. M. Ponzetto, and Andrei Shleifer, "Why Does Democracy Need Education?," *Journal of Economic Growth* 12, no. 2 (June 19, 2007): 77–99. The latter authors in particular make the case for a *causal* connection between public education and the strength of democracies.

5. John Adams, letter to John Jebb, September 10, 1785, *The Works of John Adams, Second President of the United States: With a Life of the Author, Notes and Illustrations, by his Grandson Charles Francis Adams*, 10 vols. (Boston: Little, Brown, 1856), Loc. 9961–9967 (Kindle).

6. Lydia Saad, "Confidence in Public Schools Turns More Partisan," *Gallup News*, July 14, 2022, https://news.gallup.com/poll/394784/confidence-public-schools -turns-partisan.aspx.

Bibliography

Adams, John. Letter to John Jebb, September 10, 1785. *The Works of John Adams, Second President of the United States: With a Life of the Author, Notes and Illustrations, by his Grandson Charles Francis Adams.* 10 vols. Boston: Little, Brown, 1856. Loc. 9961–9967. Kindle.

Adler, Paul, Charles Heckscher, and Laurence Prusak. "Building a Collaborative Enterprise." *Harvard Business Review* 89, no. 7–8 (2011): 94–101.

Aldrich, Howard, and Diane Herker. "Boundary Spanning Roles and Organization Structure." *AMRO* 2, no. 2 (April 1, 1977): 217–30.

Ancona, Deborah Gladstein. "Outward Bound: Strategic for Team Survival in an Organization." *Academy of Management Journal* 33, no. 2 (June 1, 1990): 334–65.

Andersen, Torben Juul. "Integrating Decentralized Strategy Making and Strategic Planning Processes in Dynamic Environments." *Journal of Management Studies* 41, no. 8 (2004): 1271–99.

Aoki, Masahiko. *Information, Incentives and Bargaining in the Japanese Economy: A Microtheory of the Japanese Economy.* Cambridge: Cambridge University Press, 1988.

———. "Toward an Economic Model of the Japanese Firm." *Journal of Economic Literature* 28, no. 1 (1990): 1–27.

Avgar, Ariel, and Sarosh Kuruvilla. "Dual Alignment of Industrial Relations Activity: From Strategic Choice to Mutual Gains." In *Advances in Industrial and Labor Relations*, vol. 18, edited by Lewin David, E. Kaufman Bruce, and J. Gollan Paul, 1–39. Bingley, UK: Emerald Group Publishing, 2011.

Beer, Michael, Russell A. Eisenstat, and Bert Spector. *The Critical Path to Corporate Renewal.* Cambridge, MA: Harvard Business Press, 1990.

———. "Why Change Programs Don't Produce Change." *Harvard Business Review*, November–December 1990, 158–66.

Borman, Geoffrey D., Gina M. Hewes, Laura T. Overman, and Shelly Brown. "Comprehensive School Reform and Achievement: A Meta-Analysis." *Review of Educational Research* 73, no. 2 (June 1, 2003): 125–230.

Brooks, J. S., and M. T. Miles. "From Scientific Management to Social Justice . . . and Back Again? Pedagogical Shifts in Educational Leadership." *International Electronic Journal for Leadership in Learning*, 2006.

Budd, John W., and Stefan Zagelmeyer. "Public Policy and Employee Participation." In *The Oxford Handbook of Participation in Organizations*, edited by A. Wilkinson, P. Gollan, D. Marsden, and D. Lewin, 476–503. Oxford: Oxford University Press, 2007.

Callahan, Raymond E. *Education and the Cult of Efficiency*. Chicago: University of Chicago Press, 1964.

Carpenter, Dick M., and Scott L. Noller. "Measuring Charter School Efficiency: An Early Appraisal." *Journal of Education Finance* 35, no. 4 (2010): 397–415.

Catmull, Ed. "Building a Sense of Purpose at Pixar." *McKinsey Quarterly*, April 2014. https://www.mckinsey.com/industries/technology-media-and-telecommunications/our-insights/building-a-sense-of-purpose-at-pixar.

Center for Research on Education Outcomes. "National Charter School Study." Stanford University, August 29, 2013. https://credo.stanford.edu/reports/item/national-charter-school-study/.

———. "Online Charter School Study." Stanford University, August 31, 2015. https://credo.stanford.edu/reports/item/online-charter-school-study/.

Chamberlain, Neil, Sumner H. Slichter, James J. Healy, and E. Robert Livernash. "The Impact of Collective Bargaining on Management." *Industrial & Labor Relations Review* 14, no. 4 (July 1961): 622.

Chandler, A. D. *The Visible Hand: The Managerial Revolution in American Business*. Cambridge, MA: Harvard University Press, 1977.

Chesbrough, Henry William. *Open Innovation: The New Imperative for Creating and Profiting from Technology*. Cambridge, MA: Harvard Business Press, 2003.

Clegg, H. A. "Pluralism in Industrial Relations." *British Journal of Industrial Relations* 13, no. 3 (November 1975): 309–16.

Colling, Clive, and Lee Harvey. "Quality Control, Assurance and Assessment— the Link to Continuous Improvement." *Quality Assurance in Education* 3, no. 4 (December 1995): 30–34. https://doi.org/10.1108/09684889510098168.

Cooke, William N. *Labor-Management Cooperation: New Partnerships or Going in Circles?* Kalamazoo, MI: W.E. Upjohn Institute for Employment Research, 1990.

———. "Product Quality Improvement through Employee Participation: The Effects of Unionization and Joint Union-Management Administration." *ILR Review* 46, no. 1 (October 1, 1992): 119–34.

County Health Rankings & Roadmaps. "Comprehensive School Reform." University of Wisconsin Population Health Institute, June 21, 2018. https://www.countyhealthrankings.org/take-action-to-improve-health/what-works-for-health/strategies/comprehensive-school-reform.

Cutcher-Gershenfeld, J., R. B. McKersie, and R. E. Walton. "Dispute Resolution and the Transformation of U.S. Industrial Relations: A Negotiations Perspective." Working paper no. 3056-89-BPS, Alfred P. Sloan School of Management,

Massachusetts Institute of Technology, August 1989. https://dspace.mit.edu/bit-stream/handle/1721.1/47207/disputeresolutiooocutc.pdf%3Bjsessionid%3DCC04 73E7EF5864D92134ADE636C6FD8E?sequence%3D1.

Darling-Hammond, L., and K. Montgomery. "Keeping the Promise: The Role of Policy in Reform." In *Keeping the Promise? The Debate over Charter Schools,* edited by L. Dingerson, B. Miner, B. Peterson, and S. Waters, 91–110. Milwaukee: Rethinking Schools, 2008.

Deal, T. E., and A. A. Kennedy. *Corporate Culture: The Rites and Rituals of Corporate Life.* Vol. 2. Reading, PA: Addison-Wesley, 1982.

Diliberti, Melissa Kay, and Heather L. Schwartz. *Districts Continue to Struggle with Staffing, Political Polarization, and Unfinished Instruction: Selected Findings from the Fifth American School District Panel Survey.* RAND Corporation and American School District Panel, 2022. https://www.rand.org/content/dam/rand/pubs /research_reports/RRA900/RRA956-13/RAND_RRA956-13.pdf.

Dolan, W. Patrick, and Lilot Moorman. *Restructuring Our Schools: A Primer on Systemic Change.* Kansas City, MO: Systems & Organization, 1994.

Dragoset, Lisa, Jaime Thomas, Mariesa Herrmann, John Deke, Susanne James-Burdumy, Cheryl Graczewski, Andrea Boyle, Courtney Tanenbaum, Jessica Giffin, and Rachel Upton. "Race to the Top: Implementation and Relationship to Student Outcomes." NCEE 2017–4001, US Department of Education, Institute of Education Sciences, and National Center for Education Evaluation and Regional Assistance, October 2016. http://files.eric.ed.gov/fulltext/ED569959.pdf.

Drucker, P. F. *Concept of the Corporation.* New York: John Day, 1946.

Druskat, Vanessa Urch, and Jane V. Wheeler. "Managing from the Boundary: The Effective Leadership of Self-Managing Work Teams." *Academy of Management Journal* 46, no. 4 (August 1, 2003): 435–57.

DuFour, Richard, Rebecca Burnette DuFour, and Robert E. Eaker. *Revisiting Professional Learning Communities at Work: New Insights for Improving Schools.* Bloomington, IN: Solution Tree, 2008.

DuFour, Richard, Rebecca Dufour, Robert Eaker, M. A. Mattos, and Anthony Muhammad. *Revisiting Professional Learning Communities at Work: Proven Insights for Sustained, Substantive School Improvement.* Bloomington, IN: Solution Tree, 2021.

DuFour, Richard, and Robert Eaker, *Professional Learning Communities at Work: Best Practices for Enhancing Student Achievement.* Bloomington, IN: National Educational Service; Solution Tree Press, 1998.

Eaton, A. E., and P. B. V. Voos. *Unions and Contemporary Innovations in Work Organization, Compensation, and Employee Participation.* Kingston, Ontario: Queens University, Industrial Relations Centre, 1989. https://irc.queensu.ca/wp -content/uploads/articles/articles_QPIR-eaton-voos-unions-and-contemporary -inovations-in-work-organization-compensation-and-employee-participation.pdf.

Elder, G. H., Jr., T. V. Nguyen, and A. Caspi. "Linking Family Hardship to Children's Lives." *Child Development* 56, no. 2 (April 1985): 361–75.

Emery, Kathy. "Corporate Control of Public School Goals: High-Stakes Testing in Its Historical Perspective." *Teacher Education Quarterly* 34, no. 2 (2007): 25–44.

Evans, Robert. *The Human Side of School Change: Reform, Resistance, and the Real-Life Problems of Innovation.* Hoboken, NJ: John Wiley & Sons, 2001.

Freeman, Richard Barry, and Joel Rogers. *What Workers Want.* Ithaca, NY: Cornell University Press, 2006.

Fullan, Michael. *All Systems Go: The Change Imperative for Whole System Reform.* Thousand Oaks, CA: Corwin Press, 2010.

———. *Leading in a Culture of Change.* San Francisco: Jossey-Bass, 2001.

Glaeser, Edward L., Giacomo A. M. Ponzetto, and Andrei Shleifer. "Why Does Democracy Need Education?" *Journal of Economic Growth* 12, no. 2 (June 19, 2007): 77–99.

Goddard, Yvonne L., Roger D. Goddard, and Megan Tschannen-Moran. "A Theoretical and Empirical Investigation of Teacher Collaboration for School Improvement and Student Achievement in Public Elementary Schools." *Teachers College Record: The Voice of Scholarship in Education* 109, no. 4 (April 2007): 877–96. https://doi.org/10.1177/016146810710900401.

Goldberg, Milton, and James Harvey. "A Nation at Risk: The Report of the National Commission on Excellence in Education." *Phi Delta Kappan* 65, no. 1 (1983): 14–18.

Golden, Clinton S., Harold J. Ruttenberg, and Frank C. Pierson. "The Dynamics of Industrial Democracy." *Science and Society* 6, no. 4 (1942): 383–85.

Granovetter, M. "Economic Action and Social Structure: The Problem of Embeddedness." *American Journal of Sociology* 91, no. 3 (1985): 481.

———. "The Strength of Weak Ties." *American Journal of Sociology* 78, no. 6 (1973): 1360–80.

Grant, Robert M. "Strategic Planning in a Turbulent Environment: Evidence from the Oil Majors." *Strategic Management Journal* 24, no. 6 (June 2003): 491–517.

Hackman, Michelle, and Eric Morath. "Teachers Quit Jobs at Highest Rate on Record." *Wall Street Journal,* December 28, 2018.

Hamel, G. "Waking up IBM: How a Gang of Unlikely Rebels Transformed Big Blue." *Harvard Business Review* 78, no. 4 (2000): 137–46.

Hansen, Morten T., Joel M. Podolny, and Jeffrey Pfeffer. "So Many Ties, So Little Time: A Task Contingency Perspective on Corporate Social Capital in Organizations." *Social Capital of Organizations* 18 (June 11, 2001): 21–57. https://doi.org/10.1016/s0733-558x(01)18002-x.

Hargreaves, A., and C. Giles. "The Knowledge Society School: An Endangered Entity." In *Teaching in the Knowledge Society,* edited by Andy Hargreaves, 127–59. New York: Teachers College Press, 2003.

Hastings, Bradley J., and Gavin M. Schwarz. "Leading Change Processes for Success: A Dynamic Application of Diagnostic and Dialogic Organization Development." *Journal of Applied Behavioral Science* 58, no. 1 (March 1, 2022): 120–48.

Hayes, Robert H., Steven Wheelwright, Steven C. Wheelwright, and Kim B. Clark. *Dynamic Manufacturing: Creating the Learning Organization.* New York: Simon & Schuster, 1988.

Heckscher, Charles. *The Collaborative Enterprise.* New Haven, CT: Yale University Press, 2007.

———. *The New Unionism: Employee Involvement in the Changing Corporation,* 2nd ed. New York: Basic Books, 1996. First published 1988.

———. "Shared Purpose." In *The Collaborative Enterprise.* New Haven, CT: Yale University Press, 2007.

———. *Trust in a Complex World: Rebuilding Community.* Oxford: Oxford University Press, 2015.

Heckscher, Charles, and Paul S. Adler, eds. *The Firm as a Collaborative Community: Reconstructing Trust in the Knowledge Economy.* Oxford: Oxford University Press, 2006.

Heckscher, Charles, and Nathaniel Foote. "The Strategic Fitness Process and the Creation of Collaborative Communities." In *The Firm as a Collaborative Community: Reconstructing Trust in the Knowledge Economy,* edited by Charles Heckscher and Paul S. Adler, 479–512. Oxford: Oxford University Press, 2006.

Hollensbe, Elaine, Charles Wookey, Loughlin Hickey, George George, and Cardinal Vincent Nichols. "Organizations with Purpose." *Academy of Management Journal* 57, no. 5 (October 1, 2014): 1227–34.

Hoxby, Caroline Minter. "How Teachers' Unions Affect Education Production." *Quarterly Journal of Economics* 111, no. 3 (1996): 671–718.

Hursh, David. "Assessing No Child Left Behind and the Rise of Neoliberal Education Policies." *American Educational Research Journal* 44, no. 3 (September 1, 2007): 493–518.

Institute of Education Sciences. *Report on the Condition of Education 2021.* Washington, DC: US Department of Education, 2021.

Juran, Joseph M. *Managerial Breakthrough: A New Concept of the Manager's Job.* New York: McGraw-Hill, 1964.

Kaufman, Bruce E., and David I. Levine. "An Economic Analysis of Employee Representation." In *Nonunion Employee Representation: History, Contemporary Practice, and Policy,* edited by Bruce E. Kaufman and Daphne Gottlieb Taras, 149. Armonk, NY: M.E. Sharpe, 2000.

Kelly, John. "Social Partnership Agreements in Britain: Labor Cooperation and Compliance." *Industrial Relations* 43, no. 1 (January 2004): 267–92.

Kerchner, Charles Taylor, Julia E. Koppich, and Joseph G. Weeres. *United Mind Workers: Unions and Teaching in the Knowledge Society.* Jossey-Bass Education Series. San Francisco: Jossey-Bass, 1997.

Knippenberg, Daan van, and Sim B. Sitkin. "A Critical Assessment of Charismatic–Transformational Leadership Research: Back to the Drawing Board?" *Academy of Management Annals* 7, no. 1 (2013): 1–60.

Knoke, David, and James H. Kuklinski. *Network Analysis*. Beverly Hills, CA: Sage, 1982.

Kochan, Thomas A., and Paul Osterman. *The Mutual Gains Enterprise: Forging a Winning Partnership Among Labor, Management, and Government*. Cambridge, MA: Harvard Business School Press, 1994.

Koppich, Julia. "Addressing Teacher Quality Through Induction, Professional Compensation, and Evaluation: The Effects on Labor-Management Relations." *Educational Policy* 19, no. 1 (January 1, 2005): 90–111.

Krackhardt, David, and Henry Mintzberg. "Power in and Around Organizations." *Administrative Science Quarterly* 30, no. 4 (December 1985): 597.

Levin, D. Z., and R. Cross. "The Strength of Weak Ties You Can Trust: The Mediating Role of Trust in Effective Knowledge Transfer." *Management Science* 50, no. 11 (2004): 1477–90.

Lewin, David, Thomas A. Kochan, Joel Cutcher-Gershenfeld, Teresa Ghilarducci, Harry C. Katz, Jeffrey Keefe, Daniel J. B. Mitchell, Craig A. Olson, Saul A. Rubinstein, and Christian E. Weller, "Getting It Right: Empirical Evidence and Policy Implications from Research on Public-Sector Unionism and Collective Bargaining," *Employment Policy Research Network* Report 2011.

Lieberman, Mark. "All Teaching Shortages Are Not Equal: 4 Takeaways from New Research." *Education Week*, December 6, 2022. https://www.edweek.org/leadership /all-teaching-shortages-are-not-equal-4-takeaways-from-new-research/2022/12.

Lincoln, Abraham. "First Campaign Statement (March 9, 1832)." Speech given to the people of Sangamo County, March 9, 1832. *Lincoln's Writings*, edited by Matthew Pinsker. Carlisle, PA: Dickinson College. https://housedivided.dickinson.edu/sites /lincoln/first-campaign-statement-march-9-1832.

Lipset, Seymour Martin. "Some Social Requisites of Democracy: Economic Development and Political Legitimacy." *American Political Science Review* 53, no. 1 (March 1959): 69–105.

Marrone, Jennifer A., Paul E. Tesluk, and Jay B. Carson. "A Multilevel Investigation of Antecedents and Consequences of Team Member Boundary-Spanning Behavior." *Academy of Management Journal* 50, no. 6 (2007): 1423–39.

Maxton, Philip J. "Embracing Both Diagnostic and Dialogic Forms of Organization Development in Order to Exploit and Explore." *Journal of Applied Behavioral Science* 57, no. 1 (March 1, 2021): 125–28.

McCarthy, John E. "Catching Fire: Institutional Interdependencies in Union-Facilitated Knowledge Diffusion." *British Journal of Industrial Relations* 57, no. 1 (March 2019): 182–201.

———. "Labor-Management Partnerships' Effects on Unionists' Interaction Networks: Evidence from U.S. Public Schools." *Industrial Relations* 60, no. 3 (July 2021): 277–306.

McCarthy, John E., and J. R. Keller. "How Managerial Openness to Voice Shapes Internal Attraction: Evidence from United States School Systems." *ILR Review* 75, no. 4 (August 1, 2022): 1001–23.

Medina, Noe, and D. Monty Neill. *Fallout from the Testing Explosion: How 100 Million Standardized Exams Undermine Equity and Excellence in America's Public Schools*, 3rd rev. ed. Cambridge, MA: National Center for Fair & Open Testing, March 1990. http://files.eric.ed.gov/fulltext/ED318749.pdf.

Mehra, Ajay, Andrea L. Dixon, Daniel J. Brass, and Bruce Robertson. "The Social Network Ties of Group Leaders: Implications for Group Performance and Leader Reputation." *Organization Science* 17, no. 1 (February 1, 2006): 64–79.

Moe, Terry M. "Collective Bargaining and the Performance of the Public Schools." *American Journal of Political Science* 53, no. 1 (January 2009): 156–74.

National Center for Education Statistics. "Table 204.10: Number and Percentage of Public School Students Eligible for Free or Reduced-Price Lunch, by State: Selected Years, 2000–01 Through 2015–16." *Digest of Education Statistics, 2017*. Washington, DC: Institute of Education Sciences. Accessed December 9, 2022. https://nces.ed.gov/programs/digest/d17/tables/dt17_204.10.asp.

Nelson, Richard, and Joseph Watras. "The Scientific Movement: American Education and the Emergence of the Technological Society." *Journal of Thought* 16, no. 1 (1981): 49–71.

Oakes, Jeannie. "Tracking, Inequality, and the Rhetoric of Reform: Why Schools Don't Change." *Journal of Education* 168, no. 1 (January 1, 1986): 60–80.

Ouchi, W. G. *Theory Z: How American Business Can Meet the Japanese Challenge*. Reading, MA: Addison-Wesley, 1982.

Pascale, Richard T., and Anthony G. Athos. *The Art of Japanese Management: Applications for American Executives*. New York: Warner Books, 1981.

Peterson, Paul E. "Bush-Obama Regulations Fail to Generate Sustained Gains in Student Achievement." Press release, Harvard Kennedy School, May 10, 2016. https://www.hks.harvard.edu/announcements/bush-obama-regulations-fail -generate-sustained-gains-student-achievement.

Pil, Frits K., and Carrie Leana. "Applying Organizational Research to Public School Reform: The Effects of Teacher Human and Social Capital on Student Performance." *Academy of Management Journal* 52, no. 6 (2009): 1101–24.

Ravitch, Diane. *The Death and Life of the Great American School System: How Testing and Choice Are Undermining Education*. New York: Basic Books, 2011.

———. *Left Back: A Century of Battles Over School Reform*. New York: Simon & Schuster, 2001.

———. *Slaying Goliath: The Passionate Resistance to Privatization and the Fight to Save America's Public Schools*. New York: Knopf Doubleday Publishing Group, 2020.

Reagans, Ray, and Ezra W. Zuckerman. "Networks, Diversity, and Productivity: The Social Capital of Corporate R&D Teams." *Organization Science* 12, no. 4 (August 1, 2001): 502–17.

Rhodes, Jesse H. *An Education in Politics: The Origin and Evolution of No Child Left Behind*. Ithaca, NY: Cornell University Press, 2012.

Roche, Bill, and John Geary. *Partnership at Work: The Quest for Radical Organizational Change.* New York: Routledge, 2006.

Rogoff, Barbara, Eugene Matusov, and Cynthia White. "Models of Teaching and Learning." In *The Handbook of Education and Human Development,* edited by David R. Olson and Nancy Torrance, 373–98. Oxford: Blackwell Publishing, 2018.

Rubinstein, Saul A. "The Impact of Co-management on Quality Performance: The Case of the Saturn Corporation." *Industrial & Labor Relations Review,* 2000, 197–218.

———. "The Local Union Revisited: New Voices from the Front Lines." *Industrial Relations* 40, no. 3 (July 2001): 405.

Rubinstein, Saul, Michael Bennett, and Thomas Kochan. "The Saturn Partnership: Co-management and the Reinvention of the Local Union." In *Employee Representation: Alternatives and Future Directions,* edited by Bruce Kaufman and Morris Kleiner, 339–70. Madison, WI: Industrial Relations Research Association, 1993.

Rubinstein, Saul A., and Thomas A. Kochan. *Learning from Saturn: Possibilities for Corporate Governance and Employee Relations.* Ithaca, NY: ILR Press, 2001.

Rubinstein, Saul, and John McCarthy. "The Future of U.S. Public School Reform: Elevating Teacher Voice." In *Revaluing Work(ers): Toward a Democratic and Sustainable Future,* edited by Tobias Schulze-Cleven and Todd E. Vachon. Labor and Employment Relations Association Series. Ithaca, NY: Labor and Employment Research Association, an imprint of Cornell University Press, 2021.

———. "Public School Reform Through Union-Management Collaboration." In *Advances in Industrial and Labor Relations,* vol. 20, edited by Lewin David and J. Gollan Paul, 1–50. Bingley, UK: Emerald Group Publishing, 2012.

———. *Reforming Public School Systems through Sustained Union-Management Collaboration.* Washington, DC: Center for American Progress, July 2011. http://files.eric.ed.gov/fulltext/ED536074.pdf.

———. *Teachers Unions and Management Partnerships: How Working Together Improves Student Achievement.* Washington, DC: Center for American Progress, 2014.

———. "Union–Management Partnerships, Teacher Collaboration, and Student Performance." *ILR Review* 69, no. 5 (July 21, 2016): 1114–32.

Saad, Lydia. "Confidence in Public Schools Turns More Partisan." *Gallup News,* July 14, 2022. https://news.gallup.com/poll/394784/confidence-public-schools-turns-partisan.aspx.

Salah, Souraj, Juan A. Carretero, and Abdur Rahim. "The Integration of Quality Management and Continuous Improvement Methodologies with Management Systems." *International Journal of Productivity and Quality Management* 6, no. 3 (2010): 269–88. https://doi.org/10.1504/ijpqm.2010.035116.

Shimada, Haruo, and John Paul MacDuffie. "Industrial Relations and 'Humanware.'" Working paper no. 1855-87, Alfred P. Sloan School of Management, Massachusetts Institute of Technology, December 1986. https://dspace.mit.edu/bitstream/handle/1721.1/48159/industrialrelatiooshim.pdf;sequence=1.

Singleton, Laura. "Understanding the Evolution of Theoretical Constructs in Organization Studies: Examining 'Purpose.'" *Academy of Management Annual Meeting Proceedings* 2014, no. 1 (October 2014): 14367.

Slavin, Robert E., and Nancy A. Madden. "Roots & Wings: Effects of Whole-School Reform on Student Achievement." *Journal of Education for Students Placed at Risk* 5, no. 1–2 (April 2000): 109–36.

Slichter, Sumner H. *Union Policies and Industrial Management.* Washington, DC: Brookings Institution, 1941.

Stoll, Louise, Ray Bolam, Agnes McMahon, Mike Wallace, and Sally Thomas. "Professional Learning Communities: A Review of the Literature." *Journal of Educational Change* 7, no. 4 (November 28, 2006): 221–58.

Stoll, Louise, Ray Bolam, Agnes McMahon, Sally Thomas, Mike Wallace, Angela Greenwood, and Kate Hawkey. "What Is a Professional Learning Community? A Summary." In *Creating and Sustaining Effective Professional Learning Communities,* DfES Research Report RR637, University of Bristol, 2005. http://www.louisestoll.com/wp-content/uploads/2020/07/PLC-source-materials_Summary-1.pdf.

Stoll, Louise, and Karen Seashore Louis, eds. *Professional Learning Communities: Divergence, Depth and Dilemmas.* London: McGraw-Hill Education, 2007.

Suzaki, Kiyoshi. *New Manufacturing Challenge: Techniques for Continuous Improvement.* New York: Simon & Schuster, 1987.

Taylor, Frederick W. *The Principles of Scientific Management.* New York: Harper Brothers, 1911.

Trist, E. L. *The Evolution of Socio-Technical Systems.* Toronto: Ontario Quality of Working Life Centre, Ontario Ministry of Labour, 1981. https://www.lmmiller.com/blog/wp-content/uploads/2013/06/The-Evolution-of-Socio-Technical-Systems-Trist.pdf.

Vachon, Todd E., and Josef Kuo-Hsun Ma. "Bargaining for Success: Examining the Relationship Between Teacher Unions and Student Achievement." *Sociological Forum* 30, no. 2 (June 2015): 391–414. https://doi.org/10.1111/socf.12168.

Washington, George. "Washington's Farewell Address." Speech, Washington, DC, 1796. *The Avalon Project: Documents in Law, History, and Diplomacy* (New Haven, CT: Lillian Goldman Law Library, Yale Law School), http://avalon.law.yale.edu/18th_century/washing.asp.

Whittington, Richard. *Opening Strategy: Professional Strategists and Practice Change, 1960 to Today.* Oxford: Oxford University Press, 2019.

Womack, J. P., D. Roos, and D. T. Jones. *The Machine That Changed the World.* New York: Macmillan, 1990.

Acknowledgments

W e would like to thank the union leaders, superintendents, teachers, principals, and school board members of the ABC Unified School District, who gave us extraordinary access to their district and schools and who allowed us to interview, observe, and collect data. In particular, we thank Laura Rico, Gary Smuts, Mary Sieu, Ray Gaer, Ruben Mancillas, and Rich Saldana.

We also appreciate the leaders of the many districts who have joined the New Jersey Public School Collaborative and whom we have studied and learned so much from. We thank the leaders of the state education associations in New Jersey who have provided guidance and leadership in growing this effort, including the New Jersey School Boards Association, the New Jersey Education Association, the American Federation of Teachers New Jersey, the New Jersey Association of School Administrators, and the New Jersey Principals and Supervisors Association. Specifically, we would like to recognize Vince DeLucia, Tim Purnell, Larry Feinsod, Marie Blistan, Sean Spiller, Eric Jones, Steve Swetsky, Donna Chiera, Mark Stanwood, Rich Bozza, Karen Bingert, Debra Bradley, and Pat Wright. We also want to acknowledge the contribution of Sam Stewart and Willa Spicer in helping to bring many of these leaders together at Rutgers to discuss the research for the first time in May 2013.

We are especially grateful for the extremely talented and committed facilitators who have been at the core of this effort, building capacity both in their own districts and in the new districts that have joined the Collaborative. This wonderful team includes Dan Benderly, Brian Brotschul, Nancy Cappola, Vince Caputo, Richard Cohen, Cory Delgado, Jim Dolan, Joe Fitzgibbon, Tania Herzog, Karen Kevorkian, Susan Lacy, Lori Lalama, Tracey McGonigle, Kathleen McHugh, Mary McLoughlin, Heather Pino, Paul Popadiuk, Scott Ramsay, Evan Robbins, Danny Robertozzi, and Zelda Spence-Wallace. Their stories appear throughout this book.

We have also been supported and influenced in this work by leaders across the country from organizations including the National Education Association (Becky Pringle, Lily Eskelsen García, Andrea Walker, Kim Anderson, Tom Israel), American Federation of Teachers (Donna Chiera, Randi Weingarten, Cheryl Teare, Joan Devlin, Rob Weil, Diane Airhart, Kathy Buzad), California Labor Management Initiative (Ed Honowitz), Massachusetts Rennie Center (Chad d'Entremont), and Consortium for Education Change (Jo Anderson, Mary MacDonald, Patrick Dolan, Ann Cummins-Bogan).

In writing this book, we drew on our more technical analyses and theoretical work published in academic journals. We thank *Advances in Industrial and Labor Relations, Industrial and Labor Relations Review, Industrial Relations, Journal of Labor Research,* and the *Labor and Employment Relations Association* for permission to draw on some of that work. Those publications benefited from the academic peer review process, and we endeavored to extend the findings to a broader audience in order to turn the research into practice for public schools.

Our work also benefited both theoretically and empirically from the wisdom, support, and feedback from our longtime academic colleagues and collaborators Thomas Kochan, Robert McKersie, Paul Adler, Joseph Blasi, Marilyn Sneiderman, Julia Sass Rubin, Tobias Schulze-Cleven, Todd Vachon, Greg Stankiewicz, Fran Benson, Justin Vinton, Wilma Liebman, Harry Katz, David Lewin, and Michael Maccoby. Doug Kruse provided critical statistical advice and Sue Schurman has been a creative thought partner. Adrienne Eaton continually provided support and funding from Rutgers School of Management and Labor Relations. We also want to express appreciation to our Rutgers colleagues Judy Lugo, Patty Deitsch, and Laura Walkoviak for their help in organizing conferences and district Capacity Building Workshops.

Funding and support for this work came from Rutgers University, the Federal Mediation and Conciliation Service, the Ford Foundation, the Gates Foundation, the Consortium for Education Change, the National Education Association, the New Jersey School Boards Association, the New Jersey Education Association, the New Jersey Principals and Supervisors Association, and the Californians Dedicated to Education Foundation.

We are grateful to developmental editor Chris Murray for his long-term commitment to this project and for editing and reading the manuscript countless times; to Shannon Davis, our editor at Harvard Education Press, for her enthusiastic support and for guiding us through the publication process; and to Gabrielle Rubinstein, for her comments and editing suggestions.

We thank our spouses, Lavina and Karen, not only for their steady support but also for their help in reviewing and editing the manuscript.

Finally, we want to acknowledge the very difficult work of public school teachers and administrators who strive each day to educate young people, often in less than ideal circumstances and without all the resources necessary to do the job. Their work is so important and often thankless. Supporting and improving their systems, processes, and relationships is the goal of this book. As Nelson Mandela said, "Education is the most powerful weapon which can be used to change the world."

About the Authors

Saul Rubinstein is a professor at the Rutgers University School of Management and Labor Relations. He is the director of the Collaborative School Leadership Initiative and codirector of the Center for the Study of Collaboration in Work and Society. He received his PhD from the Massachusetts Institute of Technology, his EdM and MBA from Harvard University, and his BA from Swarthmore College. His research and consulting have focused on management and unions that have created joint efforts to transform employment relations, work systems, and performance in a wide variety of industries. His work over the past fifteen years has focused on union-management Collaborative Partnerships in public education and their impact on teaching and learning. He has served on the Executive Board of the Labor and Employment Relations Association (LERA) and on his local board of education. His scholarship has been published in books and academic journals and has been widely cited, including in amicus briefs in two US Supreme Court cases. He received the 2019 Outstanding Educator Award from the New Jersey Association of Supervision and Curriculum Development and the 2020 Outstanding Scholar-Practitioner Award from LERA.

Charles Heckscher is a Distinguished Professor in the School of Management and Labor Relations at Rutgers University and codirector of the Center for the Study of Collaboration. His research interests include societal trust, organization change, and the changing nature of employee representation. He has also worked as a practitioner and consultant on processes of organizational development, primarily in the telecommunications industry. Before coming to Rutgers, he worked for the Communications Workers union and taught human resources management at the Harvard Business School; he has also taught at the Wharton School and Sciences Po (Paris). His books include *The New Unionism*, *White-Collar Blues*, *Agents of Change*, and *The Collaborative Enterprise*. His latest book, *Trust in a Complex World*, won the annual George R. Terry prize from the Academy of Management.

John McCarthy is an associate professor at Cornell University's ILR School, where he studies management and labor relations in US public education. Previously, he held research fellowships at the University of Pennsylvania and the Massachusetts Institute of Technology and earned his PhD from the School of Management and Labor Relations at Rutgers University. His publications appear in leading peer-reviewed journals, including *ILR Review*, *Industrial Relations*, *British Journal of Industrial Relations*, *Journal of Applied Psychology*, and *Personnel Psychology*.

Index